By the same author

GARDENS ARE FOR EATING

GARDENING WITH EASE

GARDENING IN THE EAST

GARDENING FROM THE GROUND UP

AMERICA'S GREAT PRIVATE GARDENS

The Winter Garden

THE
WINTER
GARDEN

Stanley Schuler

The Macmillan Company, New York, New York

Collier-Macmillan Limited, London

The Macmillan Company
866 Third Avenue, New York, N.Y. 10022
Collier-Macmillan Canada Ltd., Toronto, Ontario

All photographs by the author unless otherwise noted.

Library of Congress Catalog Card Number: 72–80919

FIRST PRINTING

Printed in the United States of America

Contents

1   Why a Winter Garden   1

2   Basic Landscaping of the Winter Garden   7

3   Trees for the Winter Garden   26

4   Shrubs, Vines and Groundcovers for the
     Winter Garden   122

5   The Flowering Winter Garden   173

6   Green Grass in the Winter Garden   187

7   Birds and Squirrels in the Winter Garden   193

8   Garden Structures and Furnishings for
     Winter Beauty   205

9   The Winter Garden at Night   228

    INDEX   239

1

Why a Winter Garden

NTIL my wife and I moved to Lyme, Connecticut, several years ago, I had never in my long years of gardening given much thought to the appearance of gardens in winter. If they were reasonably neat, that was all I asked for. To be sure, even a neat rose garden was no thing of beauty with its mounds of soil and bare stems waving in the wind. And a perennial border studded with stubby iris clumps and strewn here and there with evergreen boughs wasn't any better. And the burlap shelters which some people erected around fragile shrubs were really rather awful. But still, that's what happened to northern gardens in winter.

Then we bought our new home. We had been struck by the garden the first time we saw it in September. But when we moved in November 1, there was so much work to be done inside the house that we paid the garden little heed until January.

Suddenly, with the first heavy snow, we began to suspect that something about this new garden was different. We hadn't taken pains to put it to bed—just raked up the leaves and cut back the plants in the flower beds. Even so, it was almost as beautiful under snow as it had been in the green of summer and the reds and yellows of October.

The passage of time has reinforced this view. Leaves come; leaves go. The grass greens and fades. Water in the pools sparkles and turns to ice. Shrubs and flowers burst with color that dies out. Orioles and robins are succeeded by chickadees and sparrows. Fleecy white clouds give way to lowering gray. Yet our garden is never without beauty.

Just what it is that makes it beautiful in winter is, I find, impossible to state precisely. Whether it is beautiful by accident, or because the couple who developed it planned it that way, I cannot say for sure (though I am pretty certain they planned it). But these are not important questions.

The important question is: If my garden can be beautiful in winter, why can't others be beautiful, too?

I have, you see, learned a lesson. And with the zeal of the convert, I am now about to challenge the long-prevailing attitude of home owners toward the design and planting of their gardens.

Except for those living in very warm climates, Americans have always thought gardens were to be enjoyed only in spring, summer and fall; consequently, like myself, they did nothing to make them attractive in winter. In fact, they often did a great deal, unintentionally, to make them unattractive.

This attitude may have been valid in the past; but it is valid no longer.

Gardens today should give as much pleasure in winter as in the other three seasons (which, for simplicity, I lump together under the heading of summer). We are more conscious of our gardens in winter than we ever were before, and since no one gets pleasure from a garden that is dull, dreary or unsightly, it makes sense to try to make our gardens as attractive and interesting in winter as in summer.

Why has our consciousness of gardens in winter increased?

In the first place, American interest in birds has soared; and since birds congregate in gardens in the winter, we spend more time looking out of the window at them and, inevitably, at the gardens.

In the second place, we are more conscious of gardens in winter simply because modern-day houses have bigger windows, and more of them, than houses built prior to and just after World War II. As a consequence, the view of our gardens from indoors has been widened. In some cases, indeed, the gardens are, in effect, brought right into the house; and who wants a garden "in" the house if it is not attractive?

Finally, I believe that the recent, much needed, focus on ecology has given us a deeper understanding of the importance of our garden environment to our own sense of well-being. When we look at its fragile, perhaps transitory beauty, we realize how precious it is to us, summer and winter alike.

"But I'm already doing more garden work than I like," you may protest. "How can I take on a winter garden as well?"

Actually, an attractive winter garden is as maintenance-free as any other garden in winter. In fact, I might say it is even more maintenance-free because, to be effective, it has to be planted only to those species which can go through the winter without special protection. For example, evergreens which must be swathed in burlap to protect them from drying winds or scorching sun have no place in the winter garden.

Of course, the creation of a winter garden entails extra work if you must redesign an existing garden. But once

that is done, it is done. On the other hand, if you are starting to landscape your property from scratch, it requires no
more work to combine a winter garden with the summer
garden than to build a summer garden alone.

"But of what value is a winter garden in my part of the
country, where the snow is on the ground almost all
winter?" you may ask.

Snow, I agree, conceals many unsightly garden features.
It can even make a nondescript garden look pretty good.
This is particularly true of heavy snow or wet snow that
clings to every twig. But a winter garden should be deliberately planned to take full advantage of snow; and it far
transcends the run-of-the-mill garden under snow. In the
winter garden, for example, trees are selected for the
beauty of snow-laden limbs; shrubs, for the way they spear
up through the snow to make a sharp silhouette against it.

"Well, if snow does so much for the winter garden, why
should anyone struggle to build one in a region without
very much snow—say Zone 7b?" someone else may ask.

My answer is that this is where winter gardens are
needed most—and it just happens that the largest percentage of Americans live in such regions. The weather is
cold enough to turn the landscape brown and gray; but
there is not enough lasting snow to cover up this dreary
spectacle. Consequently, the only possible way you can
bring beauty and interest into the garden is to create them
by careful planning and design. This is the case not only in
Zone 7b but also in many parts of 5, all of 6, 7a, all of 8,
and at least the colder sections of 9.

This means that the only regions in which a winter
garden, as distinct from the summer garden, is of little
relevance are Zones 9b and 10; for although some semi-
tropical trees lose their leaves in winter and flowering
slackens, ample color and texture remain to make the
garden attractive.

With or without snow on the ground, this garden is a delight to look out at in winter. Though not large, it has sweep and texture and, as the jacket photo shows, a good amount of color. It is full of form. And the pair of Pin Oaks and row of American Arborvitaes pull the eye upward to the changing, beautiful sky. Note how the visual impact of the low, natural-colored stone wall and the high, white-painted brick wall changes when the ground is snow-covered and bare.

A pair of Sawara False Cypresses and a Sycamore indicate the dividing line between lawn (LEFT) and terrace (RIGHT).

2

Basic Landscaping of
the Winter Garden

AVING a beautiful winter garden does not mean
sacrificing any of the beauty of the three-seasons
garden (which I shall continue to refer to simply
as the summer garden). Even though this book flies in the
teeth of traditional thinking, I trust I am realistic enough
to admit that the summer garden will always be the more
important because it is not only seen, but also occupied
and used. The winter garden, by contrast, is usually only
seen.

It follows that, when you are planning or replanning
your garden, you must consider its summer effect first; its
winter effect second. Just don't neglect the latter. In
selecting trees and shrubs, for example, don't concentrate
so much on their appearance in spring, summer, and fall
that you fail to consider how they look in winter. In a small
garden or in the immediate vicinity of the house in a large
garden, you should use species that have year-round value.
Again, I do not contend that you must eschew the species
that have warm-weather value only. But don't use them
exclusively.

A second basic point to bear in mind about the winter garden is that the area it covers need not be so large as that of the summer garden. If you wish, there is no reason at all why the winter garden should not be limited to (1) the areas most often seen from inside the house, and (2) those seen by people approaching the house.

The latter are the least important. True, it is nice to impress friends and strangers with a lovely garden in winter. It is nice simply to lift their spirits. But most visitors are intent on getting to your front door, and fail to notice much of the garden they pass through. In fact, it can be argued that once a visitor establishes the location of a front door and heads toward it, his eyes are mainly directed downward to make sure he traverses the front walk safely. Ergo: If you limited your winter landscaping and planting to the immediate vicinity of your front walk, you would be doing more than enough for the majority of people who come knocking at your door.

Importance of areas near the house

The areas which you see from the house, however, demand all-out attention. The location and size of these depend on a number of things:

1. In which rooms do you most often sit and look out? They are not necessarily the living room and family room. My wife and I, for instance, do more looking out from (in descending order) our kitchen eating-area, my office, our bedroom, and our study.

The orientation of the house; the arrangement of the rooms; the size and placement of windows; the way in which the rooms are furnished; family habits; the physical disabilities of family members—all such things dictate which garden areas are most viewed from the house.

2. What is the size of your property? Generally, the bigger the property, the less that can be seen from the

house. In this situation, there is no need to landscape for winter enjoyment the areas you cannot see well.

However, the size of your property does not have to enter your thinking if you choose to separate the winter garden from the rest of the property with walls, fences, screens, or plants.

3. What is the lay of the land? If it is flat, you may be able to see the entire property except for those areas which are screened off. If it slopes steadily down from the house, you may not be able to see any of the property without standing close to a window. If it slopes uphill, you can see the lower part of the slope while sitting in your living room well back from a window; but to see the upper part, you may have to walk to the window.

4. What is the exposure of the garden? Is it exposed to the warm southern sun, or is it in shade part of the day? Is it exposed to the prevailing wind? Is it exposed to the street or to neighboring houses?

5. Is there a view? A view, of course, is something to be cherished and featured at all times of the year. But occasionally views open up only in the winter when the trees are bare.

6. Will the winter garden area be used for something more than simple viewing? As a rule, it is not; but if you are an ardent sun-worshiper, you may want a small spot in which to take sun baths on mild winter days. In order to do this, you need excellent protection from wind (this is usually best provided by the house walls and roof) and a full southern exposure.

Eliminate or conceal ugliness

Once you have figured out where the winter garden should be and what area it should cover, you should root out the elements which will spoil its appearance. Some of these may be obvious. Others you may be inclined to overlook because in summer they are beautiful or hidden by leaves.

Obvious uglies are basement bulkheads, garbage cans, poorly screened drying yards, children's play apparatus, canvas-shrouded boats parked on trailers, and outdoor furniture stripped of cushions and stacked on the terrace. Unsightly features which gardeners tend to overlook include rose gardens, perennial borders, plants shriveled by the cold, and other plants which litter the ground with broken limbs, late-held leaves and fruits.

But probably the most difficult element to deal with in winter is a swimming pool.

Some people prefer a pool close to the house because it is the center of family life in summer and is easy to police. Others prefer a pool far from the house so it does not dominate either family life or the view from the house. My sympathies are with the latter group because I concur in their summertime thinking, but mostly because swimming pools are not pretty in winter.

I can make an exception to the latter statement if you live in Zones 9 or 10, keep the pool free of leaves and other debris, and take the trouble to chlorinate the water regularly to keep down algae (which grow in winter as well as in summer). In colder zones, however, a swimming pool close to the house detracts from the view. If it is empty, it is a gaping, frightening hole. If it is covered to keep out leaves, it is hideous. And if not covered, it fills with leaves and when the ice (which isn't very pretty) melts, the water is stained greenish-brownish-black by algae, dirt and tannin from leaves.

Small garden pools are not a great deal better.

Importance of form in the winter garden

Unlike the summer garden, which derives its beauty mainly from its color and texture, the winter garden is a garden of form. It is a sculptured, three-dimensional garden which delights the eye in the same way a Leonardo da Vinci statue does.

The gardens with the most form are those with the cleanest, crispest, strongest lines. In other words, to give a garden a compelling sense of form you must furnish it with definite shapes. This is perhaps most easily understood if you compare the average deciduous tree with the average evergreen. In winter, the deciduous tree lacks form because it does not have a precise, pronounced outline. This is not to say that it doesn't make a lovely picture; but the picture is the result of lots of delicate lines. It is thin and rather nebulous. By contrast, the evergreen tree has strong form because it is a dense, dark blob with a definite outline.

Of course, there are differences between deciduous trees in the amount of form they possess. There are also differences between evergreens. For example, a Honeylocust is almost devoid of form because it has such thin branches. A White Oak, on the other hand, has a great deal of form of an angular nature because its limbs are so massive. Similarly, an Irish Yew has more form than a Hemlock because it is an unmistakable, smooth-edged column whereas the Hemlock has a less distinct shape simply because it has feathery edges.

Gardens with a great deal of form also tend to be rather formal. This is because garden formality, like form, is the product of clean, crisp lines. Consider the Japanese Holly. If allowed to grow naturally, it has an irregular, imprecise outline with little sense of form and a strong feeling of informality. But if you keep the Holly sheared or closely clipped, it gains both form and formality.

Exactly what is the meaning to be drawn from this by the person who is creating a winter garden? I am afraid this is less precise than form itself; but at least several guide-lines can be established:

1. As I said above, to give a garden form you must furnish it with definite shapes. I don't mean to fill or pack it with such shapes, because in that way you wind up with the equivalent of a cemetery. But you should put in enough elements with form to impart to the garden an over-all sense of form.

2. Garden form is not the product of plants alone. Man-made and other non-plant objects also have form—often a great deal more than plants. These are discussed at length in Chapter 8. It is enough to note here that almost all successful winter gardens have both plants and non-plant objects.

3. Garden formality can be avoided or at least minimized if you concentrate on plants that do not require close trimming to have a sense of form. Irish Yews, Boxwood, Arborvitaes, White Oaks, and Amur Cork trees are examples.

4. The form of many plants—as well as non-plant objects—can be emphasized by silhouetting them against a blank background such as the sky, a wall, a pond, or a snow bank. In this way, you can also give form to plants which would generally be considered to be devoid of it. For example, the stems of a bamboo clump planted in front of a wall have considerable form.

Importance of the angle of viewing

The angle from which you usually view the winter garden should influence the shape of the garden, and also the elements chosen to give the garden form.

If you are on more or less the same level as the garden when you view it, you are mainly conscious of its elevation —the way things rise up in front of you. Consequently, in selecting plants, etc., you should put greatest emphasis on the way they look head-on.

But if you normally look down at the garden, you are mainly conscious of its floor plan, so you must give more thought to the over-all shape of the garden, the pattern made by plants and walks, and the horizontal lines of plants and other elements selected to give the garden form. On the other hand, you cannot neglect the up-and-down lines of the garden; otherwise, your gaze will be riveted on the garden floor and you will get little pleasure from the beauty of the sky.

Focal points

A focal point is essential to a garden in all seasons; and it has been given so much emphasis in books and courses on garden design that there is no need to dwell on it here. But two things should be noted:

First, if your garden is fairly small and separated from neighboring properties by deciduous plants, the winter focal point gains importance because it helps to keep you from looking into next-door yards which may come into view when the leaves fall.

Second, the winter focal point may not be the same as the summer focal point. For example, a rose arbor which is the focal point of a summer garden may have scant eye-attracting and eye-holding value in winter.

Evergreen hedges

The winter garden must be planned to protect the garden from wind and from unsightly neighboring gardens. Deciduous plants cause two problems in the winter garden: (1) When they are bare, various things you may not want to see become visible, and (2) fallen leaves drifting across the landscape often make messy piles in the garden.

Evergreen hedges are the best solution to both problems. For one thing, you can plant them along your property lines to screen out the view of your neighbors' yards without giving offense to neighbors who dislike walls and solid fences, and without violating building codes which often limit the height of walls and fences (but not hedges).

In the second place, hedges trap drifting leaves far more efficiently than walls and fences.

Finally, as pointed out in Chapter 5, evergreen hedges protect enclosed areas against the cold prevailing wind better than any other type of screen.

Large lawn areas

If you live near a city, try to avoid a large lawn surface in the winter garden. I know of few things so discouraging as beautiful, new-fallen snow which has been blackened by city soot. Short of moving far out into the country, you can't avoid the sight. But you can minimize it if you give your winter garden an uneven surface (with plants, changes of elevation, etc.) and if you put in some deciduous plants to which the snow clings only briefly. The larger and smoother a garden surface, the more noticeable the soot on the snow.

Trafficways

In snow country, lay out the garden so it is not a major trafficway for people. Perhaps this is straining a point, because a few tracks through snow often add a kind of mysterious appeal to the scene. But a blanket of snow which is unsullied by man and, hopefully, dogs is a little prettier partly because it is unreal and partly because the tracks of birds, mice, and rabbits show up more clearly.

If this is debatable, I am sure you will at least agree that snow which is criss-crossed every which way by people large and small is an unsightly mess that should not be tolerated in a winter garden designed for beauty.

This small dooryard garden area is suggestive of a richly patterned carpet with very deep pile. It is a geometric arrangement of neatly sheared Japanese Yews and Common Boxwoods surrounded by Pachysandra. A Flowering Dogwood grows in the corner.

A small southern garden with the same texture carpet effect as that on page 15. It consists of large squares of Box separated by narrow paths. The squares are filled either with Chinese Holly or variegated Japanese Euonymus. An old American Holly partially shades the area.

In cold climates a smooth sweep of snow crossed with shadows of surrounding trees makes about as simple yet pleasant a winter garden as you can ask for.

Two formal Kentucky gardens (above and on p. 19) are altogether different but have the same feeling of gracious dignity and beauty.

PHOTOS BY WARWICK ANDERSON

Now a Greenwich, Connecticut, park, this was formerly the home of the late Col. Robert H. Montgomery. A superb collection of evergreens gathered by Colonel Montgomery is mainly responsible for the garden's winter beauty. At top, a view of the main lawn and lake from the terrace of the old residence (now partially demolished). Below, another view from the terrace of a small pond tucked around with conifers.

An attractive, friendly entrance area. A Canada Hemlock is at right. The groundcover is English ivy.

Handsome evergreens make the front garden of this home a delight to both visitors and the owners looking out. The tall tree is an Eastern White Pine; the conical evergreen, a Canada Hemlock; the dark mound behind the gate, a Sargent's Weeping Hemlock. A pair of fine Japanese Hollies escapes the camera's lens.

The formal gardens of Colonial times are almost invariably attractive winter gardens because they are filled with interesting shapes. Viewed from an upper-story window, they look like deeply sculptured carpets. Shown here and on next page is the Bryan garden in Colonial Williamsburg.

PHOTOS BY COLONIAL WILLIAMSBURG

3

Trees for the Winter Garden

TREES bring more beauty, in more different ways, to the garden than any other planned garden element. (I insert the word "planned" because the most beautiful garden elements are the sky and snow—both unplanned.)

To begin with, trees have enormous intrinsic beauty. (This is truer of some than others, of course.) The bare branches of deciduous trees form a pleasing tracery against the sky and very high walls. This varies from the delicate tracery of the European Birch to the bold tracery of the Black Oak; from the well ordered tracery of the Beech to the carefree tracery of the Black Locust.

The trunks have a strong, sculptured effect which shows up particularly when they are silhouetted against a wall, a pond, or an expanse of lawn. And for added interest, some trees have handsome or interesting bark which brings an extra touch of color or texture to the garden.

The dense green foliage of the evergreens not only serves as a background for other garden elements but also imparts to the otherwise rather stark, cold scene a sense of warmth. Because they stand out so clearly against leafless deciduous plants, evergreens also become in winter strong focal points of the garden.

But this is not all that trees contribute to the winter garden.

The trunks and limbs pull the eye upward from the

garden to the blue sky—the most beautiful part of any winter garden. And they form irregular resting places for snow and sparkling ice. A conifer laden with fluffy white is, to my mind, one of Nature's loveliest art works.

The branches make dancing shadows on the ground during the day; and under a full moon they form an intricate black network on the snow. When the setting sun suddenly bursts from black clouds, they burn orange-red in its rays.

Finally, trees are the playground and hunting ground for the squirrels and birds that give the garden movement.

When selecting trees for the winter garden and figuring where to put them, you must consider several points:

Problems of height and distance from house

The majority of our handsomest trees range from large to huge, and for maximum effectiveness, they usually must be placed at some distance from the house so the eye can encompass them. This is especially true of tall trees. For example, I have in my back lawn two handsome, 40-year-old Pin Oaks, but because they are only 60 feet from the house, I must almost put my nose against the windows overlooking the lawn in order to see the crowns in their entirety. True, I can still enjoy the sweep of the lower two-thirds of the limbs without stepping to the windows; but this isn't quite so perfect as seeing the whole thing.

Unfortunately, however, if you plant large trees far enough from the house to take them in easily, you dilute their usefulness in other ways. For one thing, until a tree begins to approach full size, its ornamental value is reduced; and you might well wish you had planted it closer to the house so that its importance would be increased. For another thing, the tree does nothing to shade the house from the summer sun; and I feel rather strongly that this is a major function of large trees.

In this situation, a difficult compromise must be made. The only people who can have their cake and eat it too are those with big lots—better still, with acreage. They can readily accommodate a number of large trees—some close to the house and some at a distance. But the person with a small lot cannot.

Texture of bark

Another possible answer to the foregoing problem is to plant large trees close to the house for shade, but to select species not for the beauty of their canopy but for the interest of their trunk structure and bark. The Sycamore is an example of such a tree. I have seen Sycamores with extremely attractive crowns, but they more often look rather messy. But the massive, knobby, sometimes gnarled trunk is another matter—especially when it is shedding bark or when nuthatches and downy woodpeckers run up and down looking for insects under the bark plates.

Within reason, the closer Sycamores and other trees with similar virtues are planted to the house, the better.

(Despite all this, I do not particularly recommend Sycamores for the garden because they are frightful litterbugs, showering down broken branches the year round and leaves from spring through fall. The Sassafras and Black Locust have similar problems.)

Small ornamentals

Small ornamental trees such as Japanese Maples and Dogwoods should also be planted close to the house for the obvious reason that you can see them better and appreciate them more.

Evergreens

Evergreen trees of any size, on the other hand, can be— and in many cases, should be—planted at a distance because their beauty lies mainly in their over-all outline—form—not in their skeletal parts. Moreover, if planted too close to the house, the larger specimens become a wall which not only may seem oppressive but may also make the interior of the house too dark.

Another point not to be forgotten is that the dark color of evergreens advances rather than recedes. In other words, the trees look closer than they actually are.

SELECTED TREES FOR THE WINTER GARDEN

Most of the trees and shrubs described in this book are also illustrated. In taking pictures of these plants, I made no attempt to find absolutely perfect specimens. On the contrary, I would call these representative specimens— the kind gardeners usually wind up with whether they desire perfection or not. (A plant that looks perfect at time of purchase does not necessarily turn out to be perfect when mature.) Actually, it is sometimes the imperfect plant which contributes greatest interest and even beauty to the garden.

Abies concolor (White Fir). 120 ft. Zones 5-9. The White Fir is a symmetrical, pyramidal evergreen with blue-green needles which are unusually long for this genus. You will like it planted in the lawn as a specimen or massed with dark-green conifers.

A. homolepis (Nikko Fir). 90 ft. Zones 5-8. This is another very ornamental conifer. It is pyramidal like the preceding species but very wide-spreading.

Acer griseum (Paperbark Maple). 25 ft. Zones 6-10. It is probably unfair to say the Paperbark Maple is lovelier in winter than in any other season, because it is an excellent tree the year round. The leaves in summer are green on top, silvery underneath, and turn bright red in the fall.

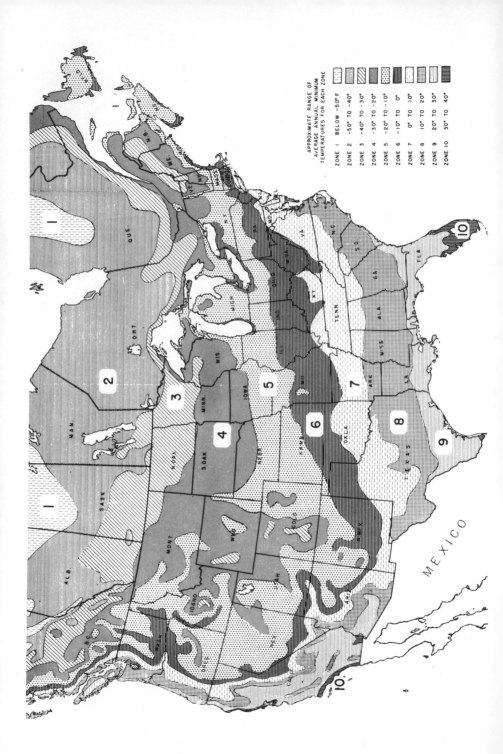

APPROXIMATE RANGE OF
AVERAGE ANNUAL MINIMUM
TEMPERATURES FOR EACH ZONE

ZONE 1   BELOW −50° F
ZONE 2   −50° TO −40°
ZONE 3   −40° TO −30°
ZONE 4   −30° TO −20°
ZONE 5   −20° TO −10°
ZONE 6   −10° TO 0°
ZONE 7   0° TO 10°
ZONE 8   10° TO 20°
ZONE 9   20° TO 30°
ZONE 10 30° TO 40°

THE ZONES OF PLANT HARDINESS

Plant hardiness zone map developed by the Agricultural Research Service of the U.S. Department of Agriculture. Each zone is split into two approximately equal sub-zones—A and B. A is slightly the colder.

The winged seeds developing from red spring flowers are showy. Still, the stout, upward-spreading branches with reddish-brown bark peeling off in thin sheets make a most appealing picture in the winter.

A. japonicum (Fullmoon Maple). 25 ft. Zones 5-10. This is so similar to *A. palmatum* that I won't use up much space on it. The main difference is that the leaves are nearly round, have more lobes, and are either green or yellow-green (depending on the variety) in the spring and summer. They turn bright red in the fall. The species is uncommon but delightful.

A. palmatum (Japanese Maple). 20 ft. Zones 5-10. Most varieties prefer sun, but some need light shade. There are few prettier trees. Certainly this is the prize among small trees. It is a rounded, somewhat spreading, and sometimes drooping tree with a delicate, irregular branch pattern. Since the tree is slow-growing and never does get very big, it is excellent for silhouetting in front of a wall or fence. During warm weather, it is clothed in finely chiseled leaves which start out bright red in the spring and end up bright red in the fall. Between times, they may turn green, or they may hold their red coloring—varieties differ in this respect. Of the many outstanding varieties, *atropurpureum* is one of the best. It is also among the hardiest.

A. platanoides (Norway Maple). 90 ft. Zones 3-10. Of the big maples, this is the most massive. Its dark gray limbs are huge arms reaching out and subdividing to form a large, round crown. It is not a tree for a small garden, but if you have ample space, it should be considered. Its virtues also include fast growth; fragrant yellow flowers in the spring; deep green leaves in the summer; and bright yellow leaves in the fall. On the minus side, it has such dense foliage that nothing will grow under it, and it self-seeds with abandon.

A. *saccharum* (Sugar Maple). 110 ft. Zones 3-8. Despite its well recognized virtues as a shade tree—an attractive shape, fine foliage, and almost unbelievable fall brilliance —the Sugar Maple just makes this list of valuable winter trees. It simply has too many branches; and when a tree attains its old-age spread, the crown is often too cluttered to be attractive. In young and middle-aged trees, however, the branches grow upright in well-ordered array. There are still a lot of them; but when you see them silhouetted against a blue sky with the early morning or late afternoon sun on the smooth, light-gray bark, they make a very pretty picture.

A. *sieboldianum* (Siebold Maple). 35 ft. Zones 6-10. This is a large-scale version of an upright Japanese Maple. How readily available it is I cannot say, but it's worth looking for. The multi-lobed leaves are green in summer, red in the fall. The bark on the well shaped trunk and branches is gray with black lines.

Albizia julibrissin (Mimosa, Silk Tree). 35 ft. Zones 7-10; but variety *rosea* is hardy as far north as Zone 5. Mimosa is a wide-spreading, flat-topped tree often with several trunks and sinuous branches. It is attractive to look at head-on and also attractive to look down upon, which means that if you have a sloping lot, you might try to locate it below the house. The beauty of the branches is accented if silhouetted against snow-covered ground or a terrace with light-colored paving. In the summer, the tree is covered with delicate, fern-like leaves and numerous pink flowers which open month after month. One problem with the tree in cold climates is that it must have good protection in the winter for the first couple of years.

Arbutus menziesii (Pacific Madrone). 80 ft. Zones 8-10. The Pacific Madrone is a distinguished tree growing only in the Far West. It has a round, evergreen crown as wide as it is high. The leaves are long and leathery; dark green above, gray-green beneath. In the winter one of the splendid features of the tree is the smooth, cinnamon-colored bark which peels off in flakes. In the spring, panicles of pinkish-white, bell-shaped flowers hang from the branch ends. Then, in the fall, brilliant orange berries appear. Unfortunately, the tree is forever dropping bits and pieces; but its beauty offsets this weakness.

Betula papyrifera (White Birch, Paper Birch, Canoe Birch). 90 ft. Zones 1-7. It is too bad that the White Birch does not grow in warm climates and doesn't do really well except in our coldest areas (Maine, for example), because it is one of our most beautiful trees. The bark, to begin with, is almost pure white (except for scattered black markings) and it peels in paper-thin sections. The crown is open and more or less pyramidal. In the summer, the broadly oval, light-green leaves flutter in the breeze, and in the fall they turn a pleasant shade of yellow. Most people seem to prefer to plant multi-trunked clumps rather than single-trunked specimens. Make your own decision about this (though I personally prefer the latter). But in any case, do make sure the tree is planted to feature the trunk —perhaps against an evergreen background.

Warning: Buy the tree from a reliable nurseryman who will not try to pass off a Gray Birch on you. Despite the name, the Gray Birch has white bark and to the uninitiated eye it may look very much like a White Birch. But it is smaller and shorter lived; and once it is bent down under a heavy load of snow, it is usually crooked for life.

B. pendula (European Birch). 60 ft. Zones 1-7. The European Birch is a more graceful, delicate tree than the White Birch and has thin, pendulous branches which undulate in the breeze whether covered with leaves or not. The branches may even reach to the ground so that you cannot see the white bark on the trunk in the summer; but in winter, the trunk stands out clearly. I have a friend who has a penchant for making tall hedges of European birches, and while this somewhat negates the ornamental value of the individual tree, the net effect is excellent in all seasons.

Carpinus betulus columnaris (Columnar European Hornbeam). 50 ft. Zones 6-10. All the European Hornbeams have attractive natural shapes and can be sheared into equally attractive unnatural shapes. But the columnar variety is a bit special. Until it reaches old age and begins to spread, it looks like a large egg standing on end. This unusual shape is as distinct in winter as in summer because the branches are so dense. In the summer, the entire tree is covered with dark green leaves. These turn yellow in the fall. Nut-like fruits are borne in hanging clusters in the summer and fall.

C. caroliniana (Ironwood, American Hornbeam, Blue Beech). 35 ft. Zones 3-8. This tree got the name Ironwood because a very sharp ax is needed to make any impression on it; but the name also suggests another feature of the tree—its trunk and larger branches are shaped like the muscular arm of Vulcan, the god of metal-working. Thus they have an unusual sculptured look which is worthy of being highlighted in the winter garden. In addition, the tree has a neat, sparse skeleton and bluish-gray, beech-like bark. The toothed, oval leaves turn a brilliant orange-red in the fall.

Carya illinoensis (Pecan). 125 ft. Zones 5b-9. Left to itself, the Pecan is not very distinguished; but if it is pruned properly for maximum nut production, it has a very good-looking sturdy, open vase shape. Like other Hickories, in warm weather it has compound leaves with a goodly number of slender, elliptical leaflets. And in the fall, Pecans growing in the South and Southwest bear marvelous, sweet nuts which· you can't stop eating once you start. (There are also varieties in the North which are supposed to produce nuts; but unfortunately, they rarely come through. Plant them for ornament only.)

C. ovata (Shagbark Hickory). 120 ft. Zones 5-8. This can be an imposing, statuesque tree, but it isn't always. At its best, it develops a sturdy trunk with gray bark that flakes off in sizable strips, and, well above ground, a rather narrow, upright crown with large branches but not a great many of them. In the fall, the leaves turn golden brown and the squirrels scamper everywhere harvesting the nuts.

Cedrus atlantica (Atlas Cedar). 100 ft. Zones 6-10. This is a handsome pyramidal evergreen much like the two following, but requiring a little less space. The needles, borne in bunches, are light green, though in one popular variety they are bluish. The outstretched branches are rather stiff and angular.

C. deodara (Deodar Cedar). 100 ft. Zones 7-10. This is probably the most graceful of the true cedars. The branches are densely clothed with stiff needles and droop slightly at the tips. One of the ways to distinguish it from the others is by its gently nodding leader.

C. libani (Cedar of Lebanon). 100 ft. Zones 7-10; but variety *stenocama* also grows in Zone 6. This gets to be a majestic tree in time, but it is extremely slow growing. It forms a narrow pyramid when young; then spreads wide with age and takes on a dark gray-green coloration.

Chamaecyparis lawsoniana ellwoodii (Ellwood False Cypress). 12 ft. Zones 6-9; but does best in humid areas along the northern Pacific Coast. The Ellwood False Cypress is a dense evergreen with soft but prickly, silver-blue leaves. It grows slowly to form a neat column not much more than 3 ft. across.

C. obtusa (Hinoki False Cypress). 80 ft. Zones 4-9. This is a large, irregular, but basically pyramidal evergreen with dense, glossy, dark-green foliage and shredding bark. It has an Oriental look. *C. o. filicoides* grows to 15 ft. and has curved branches crowded with fern-like foliage. *C. o. gracilis* grows slowly to 20 ft. and has soft, pendulous branch ends. It is a choice plant. *C. o. nana gracilis* is only 4 ft. tall; ideal for rock gardens.

C. pisifera (Sawara False Cypress). 120 ft. Zones 3-9. I have a number of these evergreens—some in a tall hedge; others growing as specimens—and the longer I live with them the better I like them. They have dense, bright green foliage resembling that of the arborvitae but more feathery; form a narrow pyramid with a slender, nodding leader; and grow quite rapidly. An excellent, smaller variety is *C. pisifera squarrosa* (Moss False Cypress). It has much finer, softer foliage which varies from gray to blue-green.

Cladrastis lutea (Yellow-wood). 50 ft. Zones 3b-8. An excellent tree for shading a terrace or planting in the middle of the lawn, the Yellow-wood has a wide, rounded crown supported by very sturdy yet graceful limbs. The bark is a pleasant light gray. The compound leaves turn bright yellow in the autumn. In the spring (but usually not every year), the entire tree is covered with fragrant white flowers in pendulous, wisteria-like clusters.

Cornus florida (Flowering Dogwood). 40 ft. Zones 6-9. Flowering Dogwood is so famous for its springtime display of white or pink bracts and, secondarily, for its soft-red fall foliage that we are likely to forget that it is a very shapely tree in the winter. I wouldn't go so far as to say it is beautiful or exciting, but it is definitely pleasing; and because of its size, it is an especially good tree for small properties.

C. kousa (Japanese or Korean Dogwood). 25 ft. Zones 6-9. A superlative tree that isn't known well enough. In winter, it is simply a smaller version of the Flowering Dogwood. It blooms about three weeks later in the spring and has white flowers shaped roughly like four-pointed stars. In the late summer, it has fruits resembling ripe strawberries.

Crataegus phaenopyrum (Washington Thorn). 25 ft. Zones 5-10. This is the best of the many hawthorns. The tree has a round head which, in winter, is a clutter of branches, twigs and thorns going in every direction; yet for some reason, I find it interesting and attractive. But the best winter feature of the tree is its small, red, persistent fruits. In some years, these are so dense that, from a little distance, the entire plant burns bright red. In June, the tree is covered with small white flowers. In the fall, the leaves range from orange to scarlet.

Diospyros kaki (Oriental or Japanese Persimmon). 40 ft. Zones 7-10. Even if it didn't produce a delicious fruit, the Japanese Persimmon should command the gardener's attention because it is ornamental the year round. The leaves in spring and summer are a dark, glossy green and they turn various shades of red, orange, and yellow in the fall. When they drop, the big orange fruits are revealed in all their glory. These hang on for several weeks. Finally, in the winter, the eye is attracted by the silhouette of the shapely branches with their rough-textured bark.

Elaeagnus angustifolia (Russian Olive). 20 ft. Zones 2-8. The Russian Olive is given high marks as a small ornamental tree because of its willowy, silver-gray leaves that move and rustle constantly in the slightest breeze. It has fragrant, yellow flowers in the spring and olive-like

fruits in the fall. But its winter value is not to be over-
looked. The trunk is interesting for its angularity; and
along with the larger branches, it is covered with shredding, brown bark of nice texture. Many specimens are
also covered with spines.

Fagus grandifolia (American Beech). 90 ft. Zones 3-9.
Given plenty of space, this tall forest monarch spreads out
and develops a massive crown supported by large limbs
with beautiful, light-gray bark. In the summer, it is covered
with oval leaves which later turn yellow-bronze and hang
on for a long time. All in all, it is a magnificent tree.

F. sylvatica (European Beech). 90 ft. Zones 5-10. Another magnificent tree, the European Beech differs from
the foregoing in that its lower branches often sweep the
ground. This is true of the common, upright varieties as
well as of the weeping types, which have pendulous
branches from bottom to top. The latter form big mounds
which are often very weird or exotic in appearance; but
because the branches are so jumbled, the trees lack the
beauty of the common varieties. In warm weather, the
foliage of the European Beeches ranges from dark green
to purple. The Copper Beech with reddish-bronze leaves
is especially handsome.

Ginkgo biloba (Ginkgo). 120 ft. Zones 5-10. Whether it
is spreading or pyramidal, the Ginkgo is a striking, picturesque tree in the winter. The up-reaching branches are
studded every few inches with small spurs which enhance
the interest of the crown. In the summer, the tree is
covered with unusual leaves like small Japanese fans.
These turn a clear yellow in the autumn. The principal
drawback of the tree is the yellow fruits borne by female
specimens. These have a vile odor; so buy male trees only.

Gleditsia triacanthos inermis (Thornless Honeylocust).
100 ft. Zones 5-10. I actually think the old thorny Honeylocust is more interesting in the winter than the thornless

varieties, because the big, wicked thorns on the branches and trunk give it extra texture. But the thornless trees are safer to have around. They have a broad, open, often vase-shaped form. Long, twisted, brown seed-pods hang from the branches late into the winter. In warm weather, the trees are covered with large, compound, light-green leaves with leaflets that dance in the breeze. Many good cultivars of the Thornless Honeylocust are on the market. Moraine is about the best. It does not have seed pods.

Ilex aquifolium (English Holly). 60 ft. Zones 6b-10; but if you don't live near a large body of water, you might as well forget the tree. This is the handsomest of the hollies—with shiny, dark-green leaves and bright-red berries in large clusters on female specimens. The tree usually forms a dense pyramid, but there is great variation in habit as well as in leaf shape and fruiting characteristics among the many varieties which are now available. You must plant a male and female plant close together to have berries.

I. latifolia (Lusterleaf Holly). 60 ft. Zones 7-10. The Lusterleaf Holly is so named because its leaves are a lustrous green the year round and grow up to 8 in. long—longer than the leaves of any other holly. The berries, however, are a dull red—not so beautiful as others. The tree is more or less rounded and handsome. You must plant male and female specimens to get fruit.

I. opaca (American Holly). 60 ft. Zones 6b-10. This pyramidal evergreen may not rate so highly as the English Holly, but you won't be disappointed by it in any way—especially since it is nowhere nearly so finicky about the climate. Innumerable varieties are on the market. One even has yellow berries. Plant male and female specimens for fruit.

I. pedunculosa (Longstalk Holly). 30 ft. Zones 6-10. This excellent, pyramidal evergreen has lustrous, smooth-edged leaves and brilliant, red berries each hanging on a long stalk like a little cherry. You need male and female plants for fruit.

I. vomitoria (Yaupon). 20 ft. Zones 6-10. If you like lots and lots and lots of holly berries, this is the species to buy. It is just covered. An evergreen with small, dark-green leaves, the plant responds well to shearing and probably looks best when given this treatment because it is rather open otherwise.

Juniperus scopulorum (Western Red Cedar, Rocky Mountain Juniper). 50 ft. Zones 6-10. This tree is to the West what the better known Eastern Red Cedar is to the East. The two are very similar. Blue Haven and Path-finder are good varieties and smaller than the species.

J. virginiana (Eastern Red Cedar). 90 ft. Zones 2-8. The Eastern Red Cedar is almost a weed tree. In my part of the country, for example, the fields and juvenile forests are crowded with them. Despite this, they are very ornamental the year round. (The only difference in them from one season to another is that female specimens have clusters of small, gray-blue berries in the fall and winter.) Until they reach middle age, the trees are slender, shaped like the conical tip of a lance and pointing straight to the sky. They then begin to broaden out a bit. Every once in a while you come on an old-timer which is marvelously gnarled and misshapen.

Lagerstroemia indica (Crape Myrtle). 25 ft. Zones 8-10. This tree is a favorite in the South because of the crinkled pink to red flowers which adorn it in the summer. But I think I like it almost better after it has shed its small privet-like leaves in the autumn. Then its cluster of angular trunks covered with flaking light brown bark give bold relief to the garden scene.

Larix decidua pendula (Weeping European Larch). 90 ft. Zones 2-7. Larches are deciduous conifers; and the kinds most often seen in the U.S. form a rather dirty smudge against the sky. But not this variety. It looks like a gossamer, somewhat pyramidal column in the winter. Small cones hang from the drooping branches for a couple of years. In warm weather, the tree is clothed with tufts of little, soft-green needles. These turn yellow before they drop in the autumn.

Liriodendron tulipifera (Tulip Tree, Tulip Poplar, Yellow Poplar). 150 ft. Zones 5-9. This is a distinctive, handsome giant. Its large trunk goes straight up and up and finally puts out big branches at various angles. There are Tulip Trees just a way down the road from me, and I marvel at them every time I pass. The unusual leaves are followed in the spring by big, greenish-yellow, tulip-shaped flowers. These give way, in the fall, to brown, cone-like pods which stay on the tree for several months.

Magnolia grandiflora (Southern Magnolia, Bull Bay). 90 ft. Zones 7-10. The Southern Magnolia forms an eye-drawing, narrow pyramid covered the year round with large, dark, glossy leaves. In colder climates, such as northern Kentucky, these sometimes become so weighted with wet snow that there is considerable breakage of smaller limbs; but this is a risk worth taking. The large flowers in the spring are white and very fragrant. They are followed in the fall by pine-cone-like fruits which are loaded with bright-red seeds. One extra virtue of the tree: it makes an excellent espalier.

M. soulangeana (Saucer Magnolia). 25 ft. Zones 6-10. This deciduous Magnolia is as wide as it is high. It usually has several light gray trunks which divide, close to the ground, into branches which, in turn, divide into smaller branches each tipped with a conspicuous, furry, pewter-colored bud. The effect is jumbled but pleasing. In early spring, before the leaves appear, the tree is covered with big, white, pink, or purplish flowers. In the fall, the misshapen pods split open to show clusters of crimson seeds.

Malus hupehensis (Tea Crabapple). 20 ft. Zones 5-8. The Crabapples have many things to recommend them, but an interesting winter appearance is generally not one of these. The Tea Crab is an exception, however. It has long, slender branches which reach up and out in all directions. The effect is of a vase filled with willowy forsythia branches which are being forced into bloom. The Crab's fragrant flowers start out deep pink in the spring and gradually fade to white. The fruits are small and of no great importance.

M. pumila (Apple). 50 ft. Zones 3-8. An Apple tree in winter can be an extremely lovely tree, but you cannot count on it to develop this way naturally. Given plenty of time, a tree growing in the open may develop a very picturesque, bonsai-like shape; but it may also become simply a thicket of branches, many of them dead. Best results are attained either by pruning the trees to keep them open so they will produce bountiful fruit crops, or by espaliering them.

The principal drawback of the Apple is that, to have a beautiful tree as well as an ample supply of sound fruit, you must prune it annually and spray it every ten days from spring into fall.

Metasequoia glyptostroboides (Dawn Redwood). 90 ft. Zones 6-10. The Dawn Redwood is a very fast-growing deciduous conifer that forms a narrow pyramid. At the base, the trunk is broad and deeply fissured; and as it spears upward, it has an unusual taper all the way to the top. In the summer, the tree is lightly covered with soft, bright-green needles.

Nyssa sylvatica (Sour Gum, Black Gum, Tupelo, Pepperidge). 90 ft. Zones 5-9. If the Sour Gum is planted in an open location so the branches are silhouetted against the sky, it makes an attractive picture. The crown is pyramidal but blunted on top. The branches are numerous and extend outward horizontally every which way. Some are slightly pendulous. In spring and summer, the foliage is dense and shiny; in the fall, it turns orange or warm red. Female specimens bear dark-blue, cherry-size fruits. The main fault I find with the tree is that it suckers very badly from the roots and is forever trying to build a thicket.

Phellodendron amurense (Amur Cork Tree). 40 ft. Zones 4-10. This tree is at its best in the winter when you can get an unobstructed view of the trunk and huge branches reaching far out to the sides, sometimes forming a crown that is much wider than high. The bark has deep furrows and resembles cork. During the rest of the year, the tree does not have a great deal to distinguish it, though it is excellent for shading a terrace partially against the sun.

Picea abies (Norway Spruce). 150 ft. Zones 2-7. When this pyramidal evergreen is young, it is quite stiff looking; but as it ages, the branchlets droop and it becomes much more graceful. With still greater age, the branches grow longer and also begin to droop. The long, slender, light-brown cones are larger than on any other spruce; and in years of maximum production, they are very conspicuous through the fall and winter.

An unusual variety of this striking tree is the Weeping Norway Spruce (*P. abies pendula*). It is like a huge, green needle, and even in a crowd of trees it stands out strongly.

P. engelmannii (Engelmann Spruce). 150 ft. Zones 2-7. This is a moderately dense, pyramidal evergreen with bluish-green, soft needles.

P. glauca conica (Dwarf White Spruce). 10 ft. Zones 2-7. If you want a small, very dense, always-green pyramid, this is an excellent one. It has short, gray-green needles. Growth is very slow, and no shearing or pruning is necessary to shape the tree.

P. omorika (Serbian Spruce). 90 ft. Zones 5-7. The Serbian Spruce is shaped like a long, slender arrowhead. The branches want to grow straight out or slightly upward at the ends, but they are so weighted with needles and pendulous branchlets that the longer ones tend to droop. Result: a most graceful tree made the more interesting by the fact that the needles are green on top and whitish underneath. This gives a shimmering effect when the wind blows.

Pinus aristata (Bristlecone Pine). 20 ft. Zones 5-9. This very slow-growing Pine is native to the Western mountains and develops the sprawling habit that is associated with windswept peaks. It is a picturesque tree of the first order. Plant it against a fairly smooth background so you can enjoy it to the utmost.

P. bungeana (Lace-Bark Pine). 75 ft. Zones 5-8. Another picturesque Pine, this spreading species has one or more trunks covered with bark that flakes off to reveal the cream-colored under-bark.

P. cembra (Swiss Stone Pine). 75 ft. Zones 2-7. The Swiss Stone Pine is a lovely, slow-growing tree shaped like a narrow pyramid with a rounded top. The needles are soft, like those of the White Pine. The tree looks as if someone had made a cone of wire mesh and had then stuck plume-like branches of varying lengths and thicknesses into it.

P. coulteri (Coulter Pine). 80 ft. Zones 8-10. Grown in the West. This is a well-shaped, open tree with wide-spreading lower branches rather thinly clothed with long needles. The cones are a foot or more long and hang on the tree for years.

P. densiflora (Japanese Red Pine). 90 ft. Zones 5-8. Perhaps this tree looks so distinctively Japanese simply because I've seen it pictured in so many articles about Japan. Certainly it is an exotic species, frequently with several trunks and a spreading, irregular, flat crown. Variety *umbraculifera* (Tanyosho Pine) grows only 20 ft. tall but is just as interesting as the species, and maybe more so.

P. griffithii (Himalayan Pine). 120 ft. Zones 6-8. A huge, wide-spreading evergreen, the Himalayan Pine is for large properties only. It has drooping lower limbs and long, soft, drooping needles.

P. koraiensis (Korean Pine). 90 ft. Zones 3-7. The Korean Pine is similar to the Swiss Stone Pine but forms a somewhat wider pyramid. It grows slowly. One of its interesting features is its large, edible seeds, which make it especially attractive to birds and animals as well as to humans.

P. monticola (Western White Pine). 90 ft. Zones 6-8. The Western White Pine is not so beautiful as the Eastern White Pine, but it's a fine ornamental anyway. It develops into a narrow, symmetrical pyramid with branches which tend to droop as the tree ages.

P. nigra (Austrian Pine). 90 ft. Zones 4-7. The Austrian Pine is a broad pyramid clothed with long, stiff, dark-green needles. The bark is very rough. It is one of the most obliging pines in the garden. More important, it is extremely ornamental.

P. palustris (Longleaf Pine). 120 ft. Zones 8-9. I have been told by other garden writers that the Longleaf Pine is a forest tree and not for the garden. But I refuse to accept this short-sighted dictum. If you have a large property with a fine vista from the house, a Longleaf Pine at the end of the vista is a sight to behold. It has a long, straight trunk with rather few horizontal branches spaced far apart, and a flat top. It looks like a lonely sentinel against the sky. And when you examine it fairly close up, you will marvel at the beauty of its foot-long needles and very large cones.

P. ponderosa (Ponderosa Pine). 150 ft. Zones 6-10. To enjoy this Western native, you also need a large property so you can back off enough to encompass its stately appearance. The trunk is straight and covered with deeply fissured bark. The crown forms a spire with considerable space between branches. The needles vary from yellowish to dark green.

P. pungens (Table Mountain Pine). 50 ft. Zones 6b-8. This is a wide, flat-topped Pine of informal habit, but not so irregular as the Japanese Red Pine with which it is sometimes compared. The foliage is also denser.

P. resinosa (Red Pine, Norway Pine). 75 ft. Zones 2-6. Often confused with the Austrian Pine, but you can tell the difference by the bark. The Red Pine's is reddish brown; the Austrian's, dark brown.

P. strobus (Eastern White Pine). 150 ft. Zones 3-6. In a family known for beauty, this is the standout. I'm not sure whether I like it better when it forms a broad pyramid with a blunt top, or when it is attacked by weevils and develops a split trunk supporting a wide, irregular, flat top. Which is to say that even when the White Pine is imperfect, it is lovely.

The needles are soft and flexible—a rich bluish-green which seems to grow much darker when the snow weights the out-stretched limbs. In a breeze, the needles flutter constantly; and when the wind blows, the boughs undulate and make soft, sibilant sounds.

P. sylvestris (Scotch Pine). 75 ft. Zones 2-8. Three centuries ago, the British navy relied on the Scotch Pine for mast timber. That is an indication that in the British Isles and northern Europe, the trees grow straighter than they do here. Every old Scotch Pine I have seen in the U.S. is misshapen in a most picturesque way. (Young trees are much more symmetrical.) Both the branches and the gray-

or blue-green needles are quite sparse. The bark has a pronounced reddish tinge.

P. thunbergii (Japanese Black Pine). 90 ft. Zones 4-9. The Japanese Black Pine is the outstanding evergreen for seaside gardens since it is very resistant to damage by salt spray. And in the constant sea breeze, it becomes even more contorted and open than it does inland (which is saying quite a lot). I understand that you can also train it by hand into picturesque shapes; but that is quite unnecessary.

Prunus serrulata washino-o (Oriental Cherry). 20 ft. Zones 6-10. Ordinarily my enthusiasm for flowering cherries, even at the height of bloom, is restrained. But when I roamed through the Arnold Arboretum in Boston taking pictures for this book, I changed my tune. Many of the cherries are lovely trees—with an attractive branching pattern and glistening, rich, red-brown bark. *Washino-o* is probably no better than many others; it just happened to strike my fancy. It has a graceful, almost fan-like crown; single white flowers in the spring.

Quercus alba (White Oak). 90 ft. Zones 5-9. No tree requires more space than the awe-inspiring White Oak. Its spread often exceeds its height. The enormous trees found growing in open lawns and fields have been spared the ax usually because they have short trunks; but the limbs are colossal, sweeping far to the sides. To enjoy the full majesty of an entire tree, it must be situated at some distance from the house; but even when it is close, you can't help gazing up into it and marveling at Nature's artistry. In the fall, the handsome leaves turn a rich purplish-red.

Q. bicolor (Swamp White Oak). 70 ft. Zones 3b-7. This is a grand, rugged tree with a rounded, not-too-wide crown. The leaves resemble the White Oak's but are not so deeply cut. They turn brown to red in the fall.

Q. chrysolepis (Canyon Live Oak). 60 ft. Zones 7b-10. This fine evergreen oak is grown only in California. It has a spreading but rounded crown.

Q. imbricaria (Shingle Oak, Laurel Oak). 75 ft. Zones 6-8. In the winter the branching habit of the Shingle Oak reminds me of the Pin Oak—lovely indeed. In warm weather, the tree is covered with leaves much like those of the Mountain Laurel. These may persist on the tree in the fall and winter after they turn brown. An unusual feature of the species is that you can shear it to make a high, broad hedge.

Q. lobata (Valley Oak, California White Oak). 70 ft. Zones 7-10. This is a magnificent, deciduous oak with huge, spreading, twisted limbs which droop at the ends and may touch the ground.

Q. palustris (Pin Oak). 75 ft. Zones 5-7. Pin Oaks grow tall and pyramidal. They are beautiful in the summer when covered with sharply pointed leaves, and in the fall, when the leaves turn brownish-red. But I like them especially in the winter because of the interesting tracery of their slender limbs. The topmost branches grow up; the middle branches are horizontal; and the bottom branches droop.

Q. phellos (Willow Oak). 50 ft. Zones 6-9. The Willow Oak has a more refined and formal habit than most other members of the family; and when it is leafed out in the summer, it has a more delicate foliage texture. The leaves, shaped more or less like the willow's, turn yellow-brown in the fall.

Q. rubra (Red Oak). 75 ft. Zones 3-8. If someone tells you the Red Oak is *Q. borealis*, don't worry. Botanists say there are two species of Red Oak. But for all practical purposes they are identical. They are upright, deciduous trees with wide, rounded crowns; rather straight limbs, and shining bark. The leaves are deeply notched and sharp pointed. They are red in the fall. Unhappily, the big acorns are too bitter to attract birds and squirrels except when other food is scarce.

Q. suber (Cork Oak). 60 ft. Zones 7-9. The Cord Oak has the short trunk and powerful limbs of a small White Oak. But the most interesting thing about it is its thick, contorted bark (it reminds me of a Hawaiian lava flow) which is stripped off to make bottle caps, insulation, etc. The tree is evergreen.

Q. velutina (Black Oak). 150 ft. Zones 5-8. The Black Oak wasn't named Black because it is so completely different from the White Oak, but it might as well have been. Both trees are giants, but whereas the White (given space) spreads wide, the Black grows into the clouds. It is a grand tree, with a rounded crown supported by mighty limbs. The foliage turns from lustrous dark green in the summer to red in the fall.

Q. virginiana (Live Oak). 60 ft. Zones 8-10. The Live Oak is an enormous, spreading tree like the White Oak, but has small evergreen leaves. To enjoy its full effect, you should plant it far from your window; but it is also very effective when planted so close that you can see only the trunk, lower limbs, and underside of the leafy canopy. The huge, 130-year-old trees on my cousin's plantation in Mississippi drip with Spanish Moss and the limbs are covered with Resurrection Ferns.

Salix alba tristis (Golden Weeping Willow). 70 ft. Zones 3-10. Willows have several serious drawbacks. They are dirty trees, littering the ground with their twigs and weak branches. The long, narrow leaves are hard to rake up. And the roots seek out moisture and penetrate drains with ease. But for all that, the weeping willow—of which this is the hardiest species—is a very ornamental tree whether leafed out or bare. The dense, slender branches weep gracefully and move in the wind; and their yellow color stands out clearly amongst other trees and offers the promise that spring is coming.

S. babylonica (Babylon Weeping Willow). 30 ft. Zones 6b-10. This is the most pendulous of the Weeping Willows and probably the best. The young growths are yellow-green.

S. elegantissima (Thurlow Weeping Willow). 40 ft. Zones 4-10. This species does not weep quite so much as the foregoing, but if you live in the North, you can't do any better. The twigs are green, hence less showy from a distance.

S. matsudana tortuosa (Corkscrew Willow). 30 ft. Zones 5-9. In the summer, the Corkscrew Willow is just another nice little tree. But in the winter, when it is bare, it comes into its own because the branches are twisted in a hardly believable way. Next time you are in Colonial Williamsburg, notice the excellent specimen at the information center.

Sciadopitys verticillata (Umbrella Pine). 120 ft. Zones 6-10. The Umbrella Pine, an evergreen but not a true pine, forms a narrow, symmetrical pyramid. The long, lustrous, dark-green needles growing in whorls at the ends of the twigs are suggestive of the ribs of an umbrella. Growth is slow.

Sorbus alnifolia (Korean Mountain Ash). 60 ft. Zones 5-10. In his book, *Trees for American Gardens*, Donald Wyman's description of the Korean Mountain Ash is one long string of superlatives. I concur. This large, rounded, densely-branched tree with beech-like bark is a standout in the winter landscape. And it is equally exciting in other seasons. In the spring, the tree is covered with big, flat clusters of white flowers which turn into scarlet berries in the fall. The simple leaves (most Mountain Ashes have compound leaves) are a brilliant green in the summer, turn red to orange in the fall.

Stewartia koreana (Korean Stewartia). 45 ft. Zones 6-10. The Korean Stewartia is one of the winter garden's most ornamental inhabitants. The pattern of branching is distinctive; the bark is beautiful—light brown underneath with irregular, darker-brown, peeling patches on top. The foliage is thick and dark green in the summer; turns orange-red in the fall. In the summer, there are 3-in. white flowers with yellow stamens. Unfortunately, this species is not widely grown; but if you can't find it, you might settle for the more common Japanese Stewartia (*S. pseudo-camellia*). It is somewhat larger but has smaller flowers; on the other hand, the bark is even prettier.

Taxus baccata stricta (Irish Yew). 25 ft. Zones 7-10. The Irish Yew forms a narrow-to-broad, upright column— sturdy looking yet strikingly handsome. The evergreen foliage is a dark, dark green.

T. media hatfieldii (Hatfield Yew). 12 ft. Zones 3-10. Depending on the specimen, this dark-green evergreen forms either a broad column or a narrow pyramid.

T. media hicksii (Hicks Yew). 20 ft. Zones 3-10. The Hicks Yew is closely related to the foregoing but forms a narrower column. If not kept pruned, however, it will in time become very wide.

Thuja occidentalis (American Arborvitae). 60 ft. Zones 6-10. The hardiest Arborvitae, this species can actually be grown in Zone 2; but since it tends to turn brown in very cold weather, its use very far north is not recommended. The tree forms a sort of pyramidal column which can be very ornamental if you prune it enough to promote the densest possible growth. Variety *fastigiata*, growing to only 25 ft., forms a very narrow column which makes a striking accent in the garden. It is also used to make excellent tall hedges or wind screens.

T. plicata (Giant Arborvitae). 150 ft. Zones 5-10. A more beautiful tree than the American Arborvitae, this giant forms a towering, narrow pyramid. The leaves are a shiny, dark green and hang in graceful sprays.

Tilia americana (American Linden, Basswood). 120 ft. Zones 3-8a. If you prefer the European Lindens to our native giant, I shall not argue. They have smaller leaves and are of more refined appearance in the summer. But given the space in the garden, the American Linden develops into a gray-barked, round-topped tree that makes a fine silhouette against the winter sky. In early spring, it breaks forth with ruby-red buds which open into heart-shaped leaves. The greenish-yellow flowers in the summer are a great favorite of bees.

Tsuga canadensis (Canada Hemlock). 90 ft. Zones 3-7. The Canada Hemlock is beautiful in the forest and even more beautiful on an open lawn where it can get enough sun so that the lower branches will survive for many years. The tree is pyramidal. The branches are slender, out-reaching, and often drooping. The evergreen needles are short and soft. One of the best things about the tree is that it takes very kindly to pruning and can be held at almost any height. Variety *pendula* (Sargent's Weeping Hemlock) looks more like a shrub than a tree. It forms a low, very wide mound with such dense foliage that you may not be able to see the trunk.

T. caroliniana (Carolina Hemlock). 75 ft. Zones 5-8. The Carolina Hemlock has all the virtues of the Canada Hemlock. It just happens to be a little less hardy. On the other hand, it is somewhat more tolerant of city smog.

Ulmus americana (American Elm). 120 ft. Zones 3-9. I know full well that no one is going to plant American Elms in his garden today, when the beautiful old monarchs that lined city streets and country lanes are being felled to right and left by the Dutch elm disease. But hopefully, some day, man will learn how to prevent, control or circumvent the disease; and when that happens, the entire country should go on an American-Elm planting spree once again.

In the meantime, let us never forget this tree—in winter, probably the most beautiful of all deciduous trees.

The White Fir is fast-growing, somewhat open, blue-green.

The dense, symmetrical Nikko Fir needs space to stretch its limbs.

Trunk and limbs of the Paperbark Maple are covered with attractive exfoliating bark.

A Norway Maple forms a bold, black pattern against the sky.

A Sugar Maple about 30 years old—an orderly thicket of up-reaching branches.

The Siebold Maple has the shapely beauty of the Japanese Maple but is considerably bigger.

Bark of the White Birch glistens in the sun and looks even whiter than the snowy backdrop.

The main branches of the European Birch are upright; small ones weep. In the foreground is a young Scotch Pine.

Sinewy trunks of an Ironwood spotted with lichens.

The bark of the Shagbark Hickory comes loose from the trunk
in stiff, vertical strips.

A cluster of Deodar Cedars has sprung up from an old stump.

The columnar European Hornbeam is so densely branched that it blocks the view even after leaf-fall.

Rounded cones of the Cedar of Lebanon grow upright. The foliage is tufted.

The Moss False Cypress has very fine, blue-green foliage.

A *Yellow-wood growing in the center of a circular terrace.*

A Flowering Dogwood with broadleaf evergreens at its base. From the left they are a Rhododendron, Leucothoe, Rhododendron and Japanese Holly.

A shapely and unusually dense Japanese Dogwood.

The Oriental Persimmon grows almost as far north as Phila-delphia.

These three Washington Thorns were covered with red berries almost till April.

An American Beech only about a third of its ultimate size.

This small Copper (European) Beech is still well clad with leaves in December.

This big Weeping European Beech makes one think of ghouls and haunted houses.

The hardy Russian Olive is often used as a windbreak. It is dense enough to give fair protection even in winter.

Spurs on the upreaching branches give the Ginkgo an interesting winter texture.

A *Thornless Honeylocust with seed pods hanging from the upper branches.*

*One side of a beginning allée. English Hollies in the back-
ground; Japanese Hollies in front.*

The Lusterleaf Holly has exceptionally large leaves. Small berries are in a cluster suggestive of an ear of corn.

Yaupons sheared to form a hedge and topiary trees.

A large American Holly with a Sawara False Cypress and a related Moss False Cypress in the background.

The fruits of the Longstalk Holly are less conspicuous than those of some other Hollies, but the plant is beautifully shaped.

Eastern Red Cedars frame my neighbor's entrance gate.

The small, angular trunks and flaking bark of the Crape Myrtle create a distinctive, easy-to-identify picture.

The countless twigs of the Weeping European Larch are a gossamer smudge against the sky.

The Tulip Tree is the tallest deciduous tree native to the United States.

A Southern Magnolia—among all evergreens it is one of the most beautiful.

The gray bark and buds of the Saucer Magnolia are especially effective against an evergreen screen. In the background is a tall, open Red Pine.

The Tea Crab has a wild, carefree look—like a girl with wind-tousled hair.

*An ancient Apple Tree framed by a small Red Cedar and a big
Japanese Andromeda.*

Two Dawn Redwoods on the William and Mary College campus are said to be the largest in the country.

The numerous small branches of the Sour Gum are a bright gray which stands out against this grove of Eastern White Pines.

Massive limbs and deeply fissured cork-like bark give the Amur Cork Tree a rugged beauty.

Branches of the Norway Spruce curve upward and are festooned with pendulous branchlets.

Dwarf White Spruces are densely branched down to the ground. At left is a Sargent's Weeping Hemlock.

The Serbian Spruce is slender and ever so graceful.

This eight-year-old Bristlecone Pine is barely a foot tall but already displays the strange shape of the species.

Despite its huge size, the Himalayan Pine has delicate foliage.

The Lace-bark Pine has flaking, multi-colored bark.

Two young Swiss Stone Pines—tightly branched and formal.

Japanese Red Pines are notable for their misshapen trunks and flat tops.

The Korean Pine is very hardy and slow-growing.

The Austrian Pine normally has a single trunk, but it is always clothed in handsome, stiff, dark-green needles.

Even on very young Longleaf Pines the needles are of exceptional length.

For all its grandeur, the Ponderosa Pine is very informal.

The Table Mountain Pine is low, wide and irregular.

Eastern White Pines in a grove wear a dusting of snow in the manner of sugar-plum fairies.

One of the characteristics of Scotch Pines is to grow more and more misshapen with the passing years.

A Japanese Black Pine above a brackish creek near the New England seacoast.

Windblown-looking Washino-o Oriental Cherry has beautiful red-brown bark.

Like many ancient White Oaks growing in the open, this one has been strung with guy wires to keep the heavy lower limbs from breaking under ice.

The Swamp White Oak has many of the rugged, irregular
characteristics of the White Oak.

Not-too-old Shingle Oaks have a pyramidal habit but grow more rounded with age.

In its genus the Willow Oak is rather unusual for its symmetry.

The Red Oak has a rounded, wide crown and fairly straight limbs.

The thick, rough bark of the Cork Oak is strangely ornamental and economically valuable.

Three Black Oaks. This is the tallest species in the oak genus.

The Live Oak has the mighty structure of the White Oak and is evergreen to boot.

Young growths of the Babylon Weeping Willow are a yellow-green accent in the often drab winter world.

Conversation piece: A Corkscrew Willow. This is a very young specimen.

The arrangement of the dark green needles shows why the Umbrella Pine got its name. The density of this small tree will increase greatly in the years ahead.

The long, straight, sharply slanting and vertical main branches of the Korean Mountain Ash form a striking pattern.

Whether espaliered or left to grow naturally, the Korean Stewartia is a prize small tree in the winter garden.

A row of large Irish Yews in a vast, formal garden.

Though generally columnar, the Hicks Yew needs some pruning if you don't want it to become too broad.

Two examples of the American Linden at its best.

PHOTO BY WARWICK ANDERSON

From afar Carolina Hemlocks look like the more common Canada Hemlocks; but they have larger cones and needles growing more or less around the twigs.

At one of my earlier homes this American Elm guarded a gate in the wall at right. But it fell victim to the Dutch Elm disease and is no more.

PHOTO BY IRVING HARTLEY

121

4

Shrubs, Vines and Groundcovers for the Winter Garden

Once you have selected and planted the trees for the winter garden, you should turn your attention to the smaller woody plants—the shrubs, vines and groundcovers. As a group, these serve the same purposes in winter as in summer, but individual plants do not necessarily serve them in the same way.

One purpose is to bring beauty to the garden. But as is the case with trees, most of the small woody plants do not do this job well the year round. The classic example of a failure is widely-planted *Rhododendron maximum*. In warm weather it is beautiful. But when the temperature drops well below freezing, it folds back its leaves and looks so sick you want to rip it out.

Another purpose of shrubs and vines is to conceal unsightly elements in the garden—compost heaps, drying yards, and so on. In summer, deciduous plants do this as well as evergreens. But in winter. . . .

In our previous house, which we built in an open meadow, the terrace was off the back of the living room. Because you could see the basement bulkhead, back door, part of the driveway, and a couple of bathroom windows from the outer edge of the terrace, we decided to plant out from the house a peninsula of shrubs to cut off the view. "Why not use viburnums?" a landscape architect friend suggested. "After all, you don't sit on the terrace in winter; so it doesn't matter if the plants are leafless then or not." We concurred with his advice and were happy with the results. But a year later, we added a small wing at right angles to the living-room end of the house. The room bordering the side of the terrace was a study which my aged father occupied for hours every day. In the winter, looking out across the terrace from his window, he could see the bulkhead, etc. clearly. The viburnum screen was no longer effective.

Still another purpose of shrubs and vines is to soften the lines of bare, or perhaps ugly, walls and fences. In this case, unless total concealment is required, deciduous and evergreen plants do about equally well at all times of the year. And sometimes deciduous plants are better because the outline of their branches against a wall is more interesting than a solid blob of green.

A final use for shrubs—and to a lesser extent, vines and small trees—is for espaliering and topiary work. Both evergreen and deciduous plants are developed into espaliers; and both may be used for topiary work, though evergreens are more effective in winter.

In other words, when selecting the small, woody plants for the winter garden, you must first make certain what purposes they are to serve. It is then comparatively easy to pick out the particular species and varieties which will serve you best. The list following is a good guide; but I'd also recommend a visit to a large nursery, one of the major arboretums, or Colonial Williamsburg which has one of the best collections of temperate-climate plants you will find anywhere.

A word of caution, however: Don't fail to take into account the rigors of your winters. The appearance of a garden is not improved by the use of lovely shrubs which must be surrounded with burlap to protect them against wind or sunscald, or which must be covered with a roof to keep them from being crushed and broken by snow or ice.

SELECTED SHRUBS, VINES AND GROUND-COVERS FOR THE WINTER GARDEN

Acer circinatum (Vine Maple). 25 ft. Zones 6-10. Needs partial shade. The Vine Maple is a deciduous shrub with such contorted branches that it resembles a vine, especially when the leaves are off. For best winter effect, plant it close to a wall or light colored fence. It can be espaliered. In the spring, the plant has clusters of purple flowers followed by red, winged fruits that stand out against the green foliage. The leaves have reddish tints when they first appear, and turn a brilliant orange to yellow in the fall.

Arbutus unedo (Strawberry Tree). 20 ft. Zones 7b-10. The Strawberry Tree grows as wide as it does high and makes an attractive evergreen screen. The leaves are stiff but handsome and have red stems. The twisted branches have shredding, red bark. In the fall and winter, the shrub simultaneously puts out small clusters of white flowers and orange-red fruits suggestive of strawberries.

Arctostaphylos uva-ursi (Bearberry, Kinnikinnick). 4 in. Zones 2-10. Bearberry is an excellent evergreen ground-cover which can spread as much as 15 ft. In the fall and winter, its normally small, glossy leaves turn bronze or red. The flowers appearing in the spring are pinkish-white.

Then the plant is covered with bright-red berries which sometimes last into the winter.

Aucuba japonica variegata (Gold-Dust Plant). 6 ft. Zones 7b-10. Requires partial shade. This evergreen has large, thick, glossy leaves with prominent gold markings. In the fall and winter, female specimens bear red berries if a male plant is growing nearby. A number of other varieties of *Aucuba japonica* are also available. On these the leaves may or may not be mottled. Variety *luteo-carpa* has yellow fruits.

Bambusa multiplex riviereorum (Chinese Goddess Bamboo). 6 ft. Zones 8-10. This Bamboo forms a clump and consequently does not have to be restrained like the so-called running bamboos. The slender, graceful stems grow upright and move almost constantly when there is a breeze. Fern-like sprays of small evergreen leaves grow to the sides. Silhouette the plant against a solid background of dark color.

Berberis chenaultii (Chenault Barberry). 4 ft. Zones 6-10. The Chenault Barberry is not quite the equal of the two species below, but it is good anyway. An evergreen, it has small, spiny leaves which take on a reddish tinge in the winter. The spring flowers are yellow; the fall fruits, dark blue.

B. julianae (Wintergreen Barberry). 6 ft. Zones 6b-10. This is an extremely thorny plant with leathery, spiny, 3-in. evergreen leaves. It has clusters of yellow flowers in the spring; blue-black berries in the fall.

B. verruculosa (Warty Barberry). 4 ft. Zones 6-10. Despite its name, the Warty Barberry is one of the best of the evergreen barberries—good for use in hedges or in a shrubbery border. The leathery leaves are green on top, white beneath. The plant is covered with small yellow flowers in the spring, and purplish-black berries in the autumn. You can hold the plant under 2 ft. by pruning.

Buxus sempervirens (Common Box). 20 ft. Zones 6-10. Grows in partial shade or sun. Boxwood is justly prized by those who want a dense, dark-green, broadleaf evergreen shrub that grows slowly to form a mound or pyramid. It also forms an elegant hedge. But unfortunately, if you live in an area with occasional heavy, wet snows, you take a chance on its being badly crushed. For protection, some people cover plants with burlap or even plywood—which does not improve the beauty of the winter garden. The only alternative is to get out with brooms during and after a snowfall and knock off the white stuff.

The shrub's reaction to low temperatures must also be considered. Some varieties turn brown in the winter if the mercury dips too low. There are, however, a number of varieties which seem to be unusually hardy and stay green all winter. Vardar Valley is one of the best.

Camellia japonica (Common Camellia). 45 ft. Zones 7b-10. Does best in sun but also does well in partial shade. Requires an acid soil. Even if the Camellias didn't flower, you would like them for their lustrous, broad, evergreen foliage. But the flowers, of course, are the icing on the cake—especially prized because they appear from autumn into late winter. There are single, semi-double, and double forms ranging up to about 4 in. across; whites, pinks, red and variegated colors.

C. sasanqua (Sasanqua Camellia). 20 ft. Zones 7b-10. Grows in either sun or light shade; acid soil. This species of Camellia forms a somewhat more open plant than the above. The flowers are a bit smaller—usually singles ranging from white to pink. But are these drawbacks? Not at all. Bloom starts earlier in the fall and stops earlier in the winter.

Chimonanthus praecox (Wintersweet). 12 ft. Zones 8-10. This many-stemmed deciduous shrub is notable only for its little, wonderfully fragrant, pale-yellow flowers.

These appear in very early winter and last for a long time. When you walk by a blooming plant on a chill winter day you will think you are in a perfume factory.

Cornus alba sibirica (Siberian Dogwood). 7 ft. Zones 2-10. The Siberian Dogwood is of interest—particularly if you live in snow country—because the bark on its slender branches turns a rich red in cold weather. But the plant is no great beauty otherwise—just a cluster of stiff, more-or-less upright sticks. You might use one or two specimens to put a spot of color in the garden; but try to place them in among other plants so that their gawky habit isn't too obvious. In the spring, the plant has 2-in. clusters of white flowers. These are followed in the fall by conspicuous white berries.

Corylus avellana contorta (Harry Lauder's Walking Stick). 7 ft. Zones 3-10. The common name describes this plant well. The main branches are gnarled and contorted in fantastic ways; and they drip with twigs which are equally twisted. The result is a freakish plant, but interesting if displayed against a wall and if excess twigs are kept cut out. Yellow catkins appear in the early spring; but from then until the leaves drop in the fall, the plant is of no great value.

Cotoneaster congesta (Pyrenees Cotoneaster). 3 ft. Zones 6b-10. Depending on their habit, all Cotoneasters are useful in shrubby borders and rock gardens, on banks, in hedges and trailing over walls. But for winter value, only the evergreen species have anything to offer. This variety, and all the following, belong in the evergreen group. The Pyrenees Cotoneaster forms a dense mound with pinkish flowers in the spring and red berries in the fall.

C. conspicua decora (Necklace Cotoneaster). 1 ft. Zones 6b-10. Use this prostrate variety in rock gardens and as a groundcover. It has white flowers in the spring and profuse red berries in the fall.

C. dammeri (Bearberry Cotoneaster). 1 ft. Zones 4-10. Bearberry Cotoneaster forms a wide-spreading ground-cover. But it will show up particularly well if you let it trail down walls and banks. There are white spring flowers and red fall fruits.

C. lactea. 8 ft. Zones 6-10. The branches of this plant arch up and outward from the base, making it useful in a shrubbery border or for espaliering. White spring flowers are followed by long-lasting, red fruits in clusters.

C. microphylla (Rockspray Cotoneaster). 2 ft. Zones 6-10. One of the most useful cotoneasters, Rockspray forms a low mound with trailing branches covered with very small leaves; it is therefore particularly suited to rock gardens and for training down walls and banks. White flowers in the spring are followed by red fruits, usually borne singly, in the fall.

C. rotundifolia (Redbox Cotoneaster). 8 ft. Zones 6-10. This tall, upright, but spreading cotoneaster is reliably evergreen only in Zones 8-10; but I include it because its unusually big, scarlet fruits hang on the branches far into the winter. Spring flowers are white.

Cytisus praecox (Warminster Broom). 6 ft. Zones 6-10. In the winter, the Warminster Broom is a dense, swirling mass of long, slender, green twigs. It makes a lovely foil for other deciduous shrubs or evergreens. In the spring, each branch is covered with small, sulfur-yellow flowers, and the entire plant becomes a fountain of color. Variety *luteus* is smaller than the species and has darker yellow flowers.

Daphne cneorum (Rose Daphne). 9 in. Zones 5-10. This small, broadleaf evergreen can be used as a not-too-wide-spreading groundcover or as an edging for flower and shrubbery borders. It's a neat, well-mannered plant; and in the spring, it is covered with rose-pink flowers which fill the air with fragrance. Like other Daphnes, unfortunately, it has a disconcerting tendency suddenly to turn up its toes and disappear.

Enkianthus campanulatus (Redvein Enkianthus). 25 ft. Zones 5-10. Enkianthus is recommended only if you are willing to keep it pruned and trained to form an upright, more-or-less columnar clump of many stems. Without such attention, it gets pretty messy. But with attention, it is happily informal. Because the stems are so numerous, the plant also does a surprisingly good job—even in winter— of concealing whatever is behind it. In the spring, it is covered with large clusters of small, yellowish, lily-of-the-valley-like flowers. In the fall, the foliage is a brilliant orange-red.

Erica carnea (Spring Heath). 1 ft. Zones 6-10. Prefers acid soil. Like all Heaths, this one spreads across the countryside and has tiny, needle-like evergreen leaves. But its main importance is its very early bloom. Little spikes of white to red flowers (depending on the variety) appear as early as January in moderate climates.

Euonymus alatus (Winged Euonymus, Burningbush). 15 ft. Zones 3-10. There are few deciduous shrubs better than this for the winter garden. It's a beauty. Above a very short trunk, it forms a large, rounded crown which is criss-crossed every which way with slender branches that have prominent, cork-like wings. Even from some distance on a fair day, the peculiar structure of the branches is interesting; and when the snow is trapped between the wings, the entire plant turns into a network of brown and white lines.

Birds find the shrub a good one in which to build nests. And in the fall, the small elliptical leaves turn from bright green to a soft red. In short, I don't think you can go wrong with *Euonymus alatus* as long as you stick with the original, small-leaved, large-winged strain. Newer strains sold by many nurseries are less desirable because the much larger leaves are almost violently red in the fall; and the wings are often non-existent.

E. fortunei (Wintercreeper). 30 ft. Zones 4-10. Grows in partial sun or shade. The Wintercreeper is a handsome evergreen vine that clings to rough surfaces by aerial rootlets. It can also be used as a groundcover or on banks. There are several varieties but the best are *radicans* and *vegetus*. Nurserymen sometimes call these Evergreen Bittersweets, because they bear large clusters of bright-orange berries in the fall. The only serious problem with this plant is that it is frequently infested with scale and must be sprayed several times in the spring.

E. japonicus (Evergreen Euonymus). 10 ft. Zones 8-10. The Evergreen Euonymus is an upright shrub which is sometimes trained as a tree with curving trunks and rounded crown. The leaves are a lustrous green in the species, but the numerous varieties with variegated leaves are most popular. Small fruits appearing in the fall are pinkish-orange. One disadvantage of the shrub is that it is extremely subject to mildew, and is also attacked by scale; so it needs to be planted in a location with free air circulation and must be sprayed regularly.

Fatshedera lizei (Fatshedera). 6 ft. Zones 8b-10. Requires shade. A cross between English Ivy and Fatsia, this excellent evergreen has large ivy-like leaves and a tendency to climb (if given assistance); yet it is essentially a shrub. In cooler climates, keep it tucked into corners of the terrace.

Fatsia japonica (Japanese Fatsia). 7 ft. Zones 8-10. Requires shade. Fatsia is a striking plant because of its enormous, evergreen, multi-pointed, star-shaped leaves. You can bring out its beauty best by planting it in front of a wall, but it will hold its own very well if placed in among other shrubs. White flower clusters in the fall are followed by blue-black berries in the winter; but since the leaves are the best part of the plant, it's a good idea to keep it from blooming and thus force its energy into producing even bigger leaves.

Hamamelis mollis (Chinese Witchhazel). 20 ft. Zones 6-9. With moderate pruning, the Witchhazel forms a reasonably neat, compact, rounded deciduous shrub with yellow, autumn leaves. But the plant is chiefly important for very fragrant, yellow and red flowers with narrow, crumpled, spreading petals. These may appear from January on—long before many other flowers appear in cold-climate gardens.

H. vernalis (Vernal Witchhazel). 10 ft. Zones 5-9. A native Witchhazel, this one blooms earlier than the above; but its flowers are a little smaller, and on cold days they close up.

Hedera helix (English Ivy). 90 ft. Zones 6-10. Grows in sun or shade. Outstanding is the proper adjective for this handsome evergreen vine which clings to surfaces by means of aerial rootlets. With it you can completely obscure an ugly masonry wall or provide a rich green background for trees and shrubs. Or you can use the vine as a groundcover. In the summer, the Ivy is covered with greenish flowers to which the bees swarm. These are followed in the fall by purplish-black, little fruits which persist well into the winter. Numerous varieties are available, some with variegated leaves.

Hippophae rhamnoides (Sea Buckthorn). 30 ft. Zones 4-8. The Sea Buckthorn is distinguished for the yellow-orange berries which are borne in profuse clusters up and down the stems of female plants. These develop in the fall, and because birds do not find them tasty, they persist well into the winter. After that, you can enjoy the thorny branches. In the spring and summer, the plants are covered with silvery-gray, willow-like leaves. You must plant male and female specimens to have fruit.

Ilex cornuta (Chinese Holly). 9 ft. Zones 6b-10. This is one of the best evergreen Hollies, whether they be shrubs or trees. The leaves are large, glossy and with five spines. The red berries are unusually big and long lasting (and you don't need male and female plants to have them). An exceptionally fine variety, much used in warmer areas, is *burfordii*. Several varieties have yellow berries.

I. crenata convexa (Convex Japanese Holly). 9 ft. Zones 6-10. This Holly looks like Boxwood. It has small, oval, dark-green leaves; forms a dense, spreading mound which can be shaped as you wish. Use it in shrubbery borders, foundation plantings, or hedges. The fruits are black. A similar plant, but much smaller, is *I. c. helleri* (Heller's Holly). It grows only about 4 ft. tall.

I. verticillata (Winterberry, Black Alder). 10 ft. Zones 4-9. The importance of this native Holly is its unusual hardiness. It loses its leaves in the fall, but it is covered with red berries which hang on for weeks and weeks after this. Male and female plants are required for fruiting.

Juniperus chinensis pfitzeriana (Pfitzer Juniper). 10 ft. Zones 5-10. The Pfitzer Juniper is just one of many good varieties of the Chinese Juniper. Its branches reach up and out to form a wide, more or less flat-topped plant. The young growth is feathery and reasonably soft, but the old growth is prickly.

J. c. sargentii (Sargent Juniper). 1 ft. Zones 5-10. The Sargent Juniper is a steel-blue, evergreen groundcover which eventually forms feathery mats up to 10 ft. across.

J. communis compressa. 2 ft. Zones 6-10. This is a dwarf form of the Common Juniper. Slow-growing, it forms an excellent, upright, formal plant with silvery, evergreen foliage.

J. conferta (Shore Juniper). 1 ft. Zones 6-10. Use this trailing evergreen groundcover plant if you live near the seashore. It is highly resistant to salt air.

J. horizontalis (Creeping Juniper). 4 to 18 in. Zones
4-10. Another excellent evergreen groundcover, with several varieties to choose from: *Bar Harbor, douglasii* (Waukegan Juniper), *plumosa* (Andorra Juniper), *wiltonii*
(Blue Rug Juniper). Some consider the last, which has
very blue needles, to be the best.
J. procumbens nana. 1 ft. Zones 5-10. This Japanese
Juniper forms a rich-green, trailing mound in which the
branches are arranged in layers and radiate in all directions. It is a choice plant.
J. sabina tamariscifolia (Tamarix Juniper). 18 in. Zones
5-10. The Tamarix Juniper spreads out to form a circle as
much as 15 ft. across. The needles are blue-green. The
branches tend to turn up instead of down, as in so many
spreading plants.
J. squamata meyeri (Meyer Juniper). 6 ft. Zones 5-10.
An upright plant, the Meyer Juniper has stiff branches
that grow upwards at odd angles. The color is an unusual
blue.
Kalmia latifolia (Mountain Laurel). 15 ft. Zones 5-10.
This is a superlative shrub for the winter garden and
the year round. Among broadleaf evergreens, its only
rival for winter value in my garden is Andromeda. Given
space, Mountain Laurel forms a large, rounded, somewhat
irregular, and open plant. The leathery leaves stay a good
green throughout the cold months, and do not curl back
like rhododendron leaves. In the spring, the plant is almost
blanketed with large clusters of delicate, cup-shaped
flowers. These are generally white or pale pink, but if you
search hard in New England nurseries you will find new
varieties with deep pink, almost red, flowers.
Leucothoe fontanesiana (formerly called *L. catesbaei*;
Drooping Leucothoe). 6 ft. Zones 5-10. In the winter, this
broadleaf evergreen turns a rich bronze color. I happen
to prefer green in winter; but you may differ. In any event,

it's a graceful shrub with arching branches which drip with small, white, lily-of-the-valley-like flowers in the spring.

Ligustrum japonicum (Japanese Privet). 18 ft. Zones 7b-10. When you need a tall, dense, clipped hedge, the evergreen Japanese Privet is a top choice. The leaves are up to 4 in. long, glossy green on top, much paler beneath. The flowers appearing in late spring or early summer are creamy-white and fragrant.

Lycopodium obscurum (Ground Pine). 1 ft. Zones 5-8. Although many horticulturists turn up their noses, the Ground Pine is a lovely, wide-spreading groundcover for deep or partial shade. The upright plants look like little, feathery pines which are topped in winter with light-brown spore cases resembling small spikes of wheat. The tiny needles are an exceptionally bright green even in coldest weather. Since I doubt that anyone cultivates the plants for sale, you'll have to transplant them from the woods.

Mahonia aquifolium (Oregon Grape). 6 ft. Zones 6b-10. Grows in partial shade or sun. This erect, spreading evergreen has leathery leaves resembling holly leaves. In colder climates, they turn deep purple or bronze in the winter. The leaves of the species also have a pronounced luster which is lacking in most varieties. Yellow flower spikes in the spring are followed by edible, blue-black, grape-like fruits in the summer.

M. bealei (Leatherleaf Mahonia). 12 ft. Zones 6b-10. Needs partial shade. The Leatherleaf Mahonia is rather stiff looking, but no one can deny that it is striking— especially when displayed against a wall or other solid background. The stems grow upright; the compound, leathery, spiny leaves—more than a foot long—are horizontal. They are green throughout the year. A prize feature of the plant for the winter gardener is its pyramidal clusters of yellow flowers in late winter. The berries which follow are powdery blue.

Nandina domestica (Heavenly Bamboo). 8 ft. Zones 8-10. Best in sun but grows in shade. Heavenly Bamboo is not a true bamboo, but has the same sort of feathery foliage and numerous upright, slender stems. It is evergreen, though in the winter the foliage may turn red. Large, white, flower clusters in the summer are succeeded by clusters of bright-red berries which persist for several months. All in all, an effective plant. It is especially attractive when silhouetted against a wall or lighted at night.

Osmanthus heterophyllus (Holly Osmanthus). 18 ft. Zones 7-10. Grows in sun or partial shade. Holly Osmanthus has handsome evergreen leaves like the Chinese Holly; forms a large, wide, upright plant. It can be clipped and used in hedges, or can simply be given a prominent part in a deep shrubbery border. In the summer, it has fragrant, yellow-green flowers. Dark, bluish berries follow.

Paxistima canbyi (formerly called *Pachistima canbyi*). 1 ft. Zones 6-10. Grows in sun or partial shade. Paxistima is an attractive, little evergreen which grows about 18 in. across. Use it in edgings or as a groundcover. The leaves are small and dense, turn bronze-colored in colder areas in winter.

Pieris floribunda (Mountain Andromeda). 6 ft. Zones 5-10. This broadleaf evergreen shrub forms an informal, rounded mound. The flower buds stand out prominently throughout the winter; and in the spring, they open into small, white, blueberry-like flowers in narrow, upright clusters.

P. japonica (Japanese Andromeda, Lily-of-the-Valley Shrub). 9 ft. Zones 6-10. Of the many shrubs we have planted since moving to Lyme, we have relied more heavily on the Japanese Andromeda than anything else. It is a top-notch evergreen, almost as wide as high, and clothed all the way to the ground with lustrous elliptical leaves. These are overlaid with sprays of tiny flower buds at the end of short, red stems which give the entire plant a rosy hue in winter. In the spring, the shrub is sheathed with pendulous clusters of creamy-white flowers like those of the lily-of-the-valley. New leaves in the spring start out a delightful reddish-bronze and then turn medium green.

Pinus mugo mughus (Mugo Pine). 8 ft. Zones 2-9. The Mugo Pine is a dense, low, spreading shrub which forms attractive irregular mounds. The needles are 3 in. long, dark green and stiff. In the spring, the numerous white candles which grow upright from the plant make it look something like a pincushion.

Photinia fraseri (Fraser Photinia). 10 ft. Zones 7b-10. This rounded evergreen has glossy leaves which are dark green on top, medium green beneath. In late winter, the new growth which is put out is a showy red. In warm weather white flowers are followed by red berries. The shrub is good for espaliering.

Phyllostachys aureosulcata (Yellow Groove Bamboo). 15 ft. Zones 6-10. This unusually hardy evergreen Bamboo has slender, stiff stems which show off to best advantage in front of a fairly solid background. The young stems are green with yellow grooves. Unfortunately, the plant spreads rapidly over a wide area unless you keep the rhizomes cut back.

Podocarpus macrophyllus maki (Yew Podocarpus, Shrubby Yew Pine). 10 ft. Zones 8-10. Grows in sun or partial shade. This Podocarpus resembles a yew with unusually long leaves of a slightly lighter green. It is an excellent shrub which can be used as a specimen plant, in a hedge, or in a container. Slow growing, it takes kindly to shearing.

Pyracantha coccinea lalandii (Firethorn). 20 ft. Zones 6-10. In the coldest weather Pyracantha may lose its leaves, but it is certainly evergreen from Zone 6b south. It is an outstanding shrub for espaliering, and shows off to best advantage when handled in this way; but it can be allowed to develop into a large, somewhat sprawling, foundation or border plant. It has small clusters of white flowers in the spring. These are relatively insignificant; but the masses of bright, orange-red berries that follow in the autumn are something else again. If you are lucky, the birds won't notice them and they will hang on the plant through the fall and into the winter. If you're not lucky, they will be gobbled up in a few hours; on the other hand, you will be amused (between tears) to see how frantic a flock of birds can get.

Rhododendron. I am not enthusiastic about deciduous Rhododendrons for any winter garden because their branching structure is neither interesting nor pretty. And evergreen Rhododendrons react in such depressing fashion to freezing temperatures that I don't recommend them for the winter garden north of Zone 8. In that zone, you can use any variety that a reliable local nurseryman recommends.

Evergreen Azaleas have much smaller leaves than Rhododendrons and do not grow so far north; consequently, their reaction to low temperatures does not command attention, and they can find a happy place in winter gardens from Zones 7 to 9. The Indian, Kurume and Glen Dale hybrids are among the best for beauty of foliage and flower.

Sasa palmata (Palmate Bamboo). 5 ft. Zones 6a-10. This running (spreading) Bamboo has unusually large, long leaves which grow out like fingers from the graceful stems. In coldest areas, the leaves may turn yellow in the winter; but usually they remain green on top, silvery underneath. Silhouette the plant against a solid background so you can enjoy its movement in the wind.

Skimmia reevesiana (Reeves Skimmia). 2 ft. Zones 7b-
10. Requires shade. This is a nice little broadleaf evergreen
with many possible uses. It is low and rounded; well
clothed with dark-green leaves in neat array. Fragrant,
white flowers in the spring are followed by dull-red, holly-
like fruits which last through the winter. Plant male and
female specimens for fruit.

Stranvaesia davidiana. 20 ft. Zones 7b-10. This wide-
spreading, informal, broadleaf evergreen is at its best in
the early winter, when the leaves turn purple or bronze
and the berry clusters are a showy red. In the spring, the
plant has clusters of white flowers and the new leaves are
tinged with red.

Taxus cuspidata (Japanese Yew). Up to 20 ft., depending on variety. Zones 5-10. The Yews, with their short,
dark-green needles, are a mainstay of the winter garden if
the deer will just leave them alone. Most grow about as
wide as they are high or even wider, and need to be pruned
regularly to keep them in bounds. Happily, they respond
well to shearing; are ideal for topiary work; and make
splendid espaliers.

Ternstroemia gymnanthera (sometimes identified as
T. japonica). 10 ft. Zones 8-10. Requires acid soil. This
broadleaf evergreen has lovely, leathery foliage which
takes on purplish-red tints in winter if growing in the sun.
(In partial shade, in which it also thrives, the foliage is
usually dark green.) In the summer, the shrub has small,
fragrant, creamy-yellow flowers. These are followed by
orange-red, holly-like berries.

Vaccinium corymbosum (Highbush Blueberry). 10 ft.
Zones 5-7. Requires acid soil. The dense-branching habit
of the Blueberry is surprisingly attractive in winter, especially after a new-fallen snow; and the red color of the
twigs adds to the picture. In the spring, the plant is
covered with dainty, little, white to pink flowers. These are

followed, during the summer, by delicious blueberries. Then, in the fall, the foliage turns scarlet.

Viburnum rhytidophyllum (Leatherleaf Viburnum). 9 ft. Zones 7-10. Needs protection from wind. The long, wrinkled, leathery leaves of this rounded shrub last the winter through except in the coldest years. The flowers appearing in the spring, in large, flat clusters, are yellowish white. The fruits in the fall turn from red to black.

Vinca minor (Periwinkle, Myrtle). 8 in. Zones 5-10. Grows in sun or shade. No groundcover can match the Periwinkle for year-round value. In freezing weather, when Pachysandra curls up and looks sick, Periwinkle looks as green and robust as in the middle of summer. In the spring, it is dotted with bright blue flowers. The only thing I have ever known to bother a carpet of Periwinkle is a dog that persists in following a set trail through it. This wears a bare path across the carpet—but then, it will wear a path in other groundcovers, too.

Bearberry is a low, spreading, tough evergreen groundcover.

The spiny leaves of the Chenault Barberry become reddish in winter.

A trio of Gold-Dust Plants with yellow-mottled evergreen foliage. Behind them is an Evergreen Dogwood.

The Wintergreen Barberry is thorny enough to turn back animals as well as humans.

A Common Boxwood in a bed of Pachysandra.

PHOTO BY WARWICK ANDERSON

Though not particularly pretty in a black and white photograph, this mass of Siberian Dogwood makes a bright red spot in the winter landscape.

In winter, when Harry Lauder's Walking Stick is bare, it probably stimulates more comment than any other plant.

Bearberry Cotoneaster in one of its best roles: As a trailer in the rock garden.

The bright green of Warminster Broom twigs is a rare and welcome color in the winter garden.

Spearing up through the snow are Spring Heath and an assortment of Heathers.

After a winter shower, the angular branches of the Winged
Euonymus glisten in the sun.

Wintercreeper, here covering a gate post, is an excellent climbing vine and also a groundcover. The hedge is composed of Canada Hemlocks.

The large lobed leaves of the Japanese Fatsia have a tropical look, but the plant lives outdoors as far north as Zone 8.

Fatshedera has the leaves of the Fatsia, the climbing tendencies of the English Ivy.

Two forms of English Ivy: The upper leaves are big, bright green and roughly heart-shaped. The lower leaves are smaller, lobed and dark purplish-green.

Chinese Holly is a gorgeous evergreen with big red berries and lustrous, five-spined leaves.

*Heller's Holly dusted with snow borders a brick terrace. An
American Holly grows beyond the railing.*

A *magnificent specimen of the Winterberry forms a fountain of red berries.*

A mass of Pfitzer Junipers. The plants are heavy with small, powder-blue berries.

A splendid groundcover for a sunny hillside—Sargent Juniper.

Waukegan Juniper forms a dense, thick mat in a sunny spot out beyond the branches of an old White Pine.

Close-up of a Meyer Juniper with stiff, upreaching branches.

Mountain Laurel grows into a large, somewhat irregular ever-green that shrugs off winter cold. An American Arborvitae grows beside the entrance.

Compact Mountain Laurel—a rather rare but choice form of a superb winter shrub. At left is an unusual form of Japanese Holly.

A young specimen of Japanese Privet, a dense, lustrous evergreen.

A carpet of Ground Pine raises its feathery leaves and small spore spikes above the snow.

This Oregon Grape, photographed in Boston in early February, was a glistening, pure purple.

An upright Leatherleaf Mahonia is laden with developing flower buds in late winter.

Although badly pruned, this Heavenly Bamboo displays much of the airy grace characterizing this plant.

Foliage of the rounded Holly Osmanthus looks almost exactly like that of a true Holly.

An excellent, small-leaved evergreen groundcover for sun or partial shade—Paxistima.

On the Mountain Andromeda the sprays of latent flower buds grow upright.

On the Japanese Andromeda the bud sprays are spreading
and drooping.

Foliage of a large Japanese Andromeda glistens in the sun. Sycamores in the background are effective winter trees but bad litterbugs.

Mugo Pines build into dense, spreading, tufted mounds.

Bamboo in the north? Yes. This big clump of Sasa Bamboos is in the Arnold Arboretum, Boston.

Graceful Yellow-groove Bamboo surrounds the trunk of a Loblolly Pine.

Evergreen Fraser Photinia is especially notable for its new red growths.

Espaliered Pyracanthas on the chimney of the Greenwich, Connecticut, Garden Center—formerly a home—rise to unusual heights.

Informal Stranvaesia has bronze or purplish leaves, red fruits.

Upright Ternstroemia—another good broadleaf evergreen for southern gardens.

Crooked branches of the Highbush Blueberry form an interesting pattern. The twigs are reddish.

Long leaves cover the rounded Leatherleaf Viburnum like narrow shingles.

5

The Flowering Winter Garden

FLOWERS in winter? Indeed, why not. I don't promise them if you live in Zones 3 or 4. But from Zone 5 southward, it is possible to have bloom—if not in every winter month—in at least a couple of them.

Naturally, the warmer climates will have more bloom, with greater variety, than cold climates. Bloom will usually come later in the year in colder climates. And bloom in all climates will be affected by the severity of the winter. These variables make it impossible to be precise about what you can expect when. But this very uncertainty adds to the fun of putting in plants in the hope of having a pretty flower winking at you through the snow.

Establishing the proper conditions for winter bloom

Getting certain flowers to bloom in the winter is, in good part, a matter of creating conditions that encourage bloom. If you let Nature run the whole show, flowering will generally be delayed until February, March or April (depending on where you live). But if you take a hand, flowering can usually be advanced several weeks, except in very rugged winters.

With the exception of Camellias and Hellebores, plants need three things to bloom in winter.

1. The first is *warmth*, and the best source of this is the sun. Give flowering plants a southern exposure so they will be warmed by the sun from the time it rises in the southeast in the morning until it sets in the southwest in the evening. The ideal location, particularly for low-growing plants such as perennials and bulbs, is right in front of a furnace chimney on the south side of the house, because the heat escaping through the masonry adds to the sun's heat and forces the plants to bloom days earlier than they would otherwise. Another, almost-as-good location is right in front of any south-facing wall because it reflects the sun's heat, and raises the temperature of the soil at its base.

(Camellias should be given a northern or western exposure, or should be planted under trees, so they will warm up slowly on winter mornings and thus escape serious cold damage. Hellebores also require a northern, western, or eastern exposure because they need shade to do their best.)

2. The second thing that all plants, including Camellias and Hellebores, require is all possible *protection from late frosts*. This simply means that you must plant them in a location with good air drainage: Avoid low spots in which cold air settles.

3. The third thing that all plants require is *protection from cold prevailing winds*. This is usually best provided by the high walls of a house, garage or other building. Such protection is not available on all properties, of course, and if that is true in your case, then you must provide protection by means of shrubbery, garden walls, or fences. To do this properly, it is necessary to understand how wind reacts when it meets a barrier.

If the barrier is a solid wall or fence, the wind sails up over it like an Olympic hurdler, comes down on the other side, and keeps on going. This means that the only plants protected by the wall are those in its immediate lee. The exact width of the protected area depends on the height of the wall.

If the barrier used to control the wind is porous, however, the effect is quite different. Instead of sailing over the top, the wind hits the barrier head on and comes through the holes. But by the time it emerges on the other side, its force has been dissipated. Thus the plants which are a distance from the barrier receive as much protection as those close to it.

It should be clear from this that the type of wind screen you erect to protect winter flowers depends on the size of the planted area. If this is very small, a high, solid wall or fence will probably do the job. But if the area is large, you should build a wall of pierced-concrete blocks; or a fence with spaces between the boards; or you should plant a hedge or shrubbery border. The best of these alternatives is the last. Plants, whether used in a clipped hedge or an informal border, break up the wind more effectively than anything else. The best plants to use are, in descending order; needled evergreens, broadleaf evergreens, and dense deciduous plants such as Privet or Enkianthus.

SELECTED FLOWERS FOR THE WINTER GARDEN

Hellebores. Of the several plants which bloom in the winter, the Hellebores are outstanding because they grow in Zones 5 or 6 (depending on the species) southward to 10, and bloom in the dead of winter almost everywhere. In addition, they require little attention. Just plant them in a shady spot in soil containing a large amount of humus. Water them in dry spells during the summer. Give them a light dose of fertilizer in October or simply mulch them with leafmold, peat, or other organic material. Since they do not like to be disturbed too much, divide them only when they become crowded with flower stalks.

The most widely known Hellebore is the Christmas Rose (*Helleborus niger*). Its common name stems from the fact that it almost never fails to bloom at Christmas in moderate climates, and for several months thereafter. Like other Hellebores, this elegant, 18-in., evergreen plant has basal clumps of large, compound leaves with leaflets arranged in the shape of a fan. The showy, five-petaled, single flowers, about 2 in. in diameter, start out white and gradually, over a period of several weeks, turn dusky pink and then green. A single, well established plant may have as many as 30 blooms.

The Lenten Rose (*H. orientalis*) is very similar but starts blooming about February or March and continues past Easter. It also takes more kindly to transplanting, and does better in mild climates. Flower colors range from purple to rich brown, to rose to white. Some varieties are spotted with deep red.

Another excellent Hellebore is *H. foetidus*, but unfortunately, it is difficult to find. The 1-in. flowers are pale green with purple edges. They usually appear along with the Lenten rose, but occasionally they are considerably earlier.

Other perennials. The dates given in the following descriptions of perennials and bulbs are roughly what you can expect if you live in Zone 7 and southward.

Adonis amurensis. Zones 6-8. This is a 1-ft. plant with feathery foliage and bright-yellow, buttercup-like flowers as much as 2 in. across. They appear in March. The plant grows in sun or light shade.

Bergenia ligulata. Zones 6-10. A choice plant, 1 ft. high, this March bloomer has nodding clusters of white, pink, or purple flowers and very large, almost round, hairy-edged leaves which are evergreen in warmer climates. Grows in partial shade.

Petasites fragrans (Winter Heliotrope). Zones 7-10. Winter Heliotrope is a spreading, 8-in., evergreen perennial with small flowers appearing in March. These have a vanilla-like fragrance; range from purple to whitish in color.

Primula denticulata. Zones 5-8. There are other species of primula which bloom ahead of *denticulata*, but they grow only in the warm climates where many kinds of flowers bloom in winter. This Primula blooms in March and has dense, round clusters of white, pink, red, or purple flowers with white eyes. The plant grows about 1 ft. high in boggy or damp, humusy soil.

Pulmonaria angustifolia (Cowslip Lungwort). Zones 4-10. This 1-ft. perennial produces funnel-shaped blue flowers in clusters in March. It grows in the shade.

P. saccharata (Bethlehem Sage). Zones 4-10. Another shade-loving plant, this one grows to 18 in. and forms a clump about 2 ft. across. The leaves are spotted. The funnel-shaped flowers are purplish, pink, white, or blue. They appear in March.

Pulsatilla vernalis. Zones 7-10. A charming little plant, no more than 6 in. high, this has feathery, evergreen leaves covered with yellow hairs. In March, it puts out silky, yellow buds which open into golden blossoms 2 in. across.

Bulbs. *Anemone blanda* (Sapphire Windflower). Zones 7-10. This tuberous-rooted Anemone grows to about 6 in. and has dark-blue, daisy-like flowers in late March. White- and pink-flowered varieties are also available. All require partial shade.

Bulbocodium vernum (Spring Meadow Saffron). Zones 4-8. This rugged, 4-in., bulbous plant brightens late February and March days with its raspberry-colored, crocus-like blooms. The foliage comes after the flowers. It does best in the sun, but also grows in light shade.

Chionodoxa luciliae (Glory of the Snow). Zones 3-8. There are several other excellent species of Chionodoxa, but this is the most generally available. It is a charming, bulbous plant, 8 in. high, with loose clusters of six-pointed, star-like flowers of brilliant blue with white centers. March is the usual blooming time. Variety *gigantea* is also blue and extra big; *alba* is white.

Crocus aureus. Zones 3-8. When the tedium of winter gets you down, the obliging little Crocuses come to the rescue. This is one of the earliest, often flowering in February. It is a rich yellow-orange.

C. biflorus (Scotch Crocus). Zones 3-8. The species has white flowers with bluish-purple stripes on the outside of the petals. It blooms in March. There are several varieties, including an excellent pure white named White Lady.

C. chrysanthus. Zones 3-8. A lovely species starting to bloom in February, *chrysanthus* has a great many varieties in white, yellow, blue or lavender.

C. imperati. Zones 3-8. This choice species has February flowers in two shades of violet.

C. longiflorus. Zones 5-8. In the fall, when you feel depressed about the approach of winter, this Crocus will lift your spirits with its violet flowers with yellow and red centers. Flowering starts in early November and continues until the middle of December.

C. sieberi atticus. Zones 3-8. Another extremely early Crocus, this one has been known to bloom in late December. It is purple with a yellow throat.

C. susianus (Cloth of Gold). Zones 3-8. Look for the Cloth of Gold along in March. It has yellow flowers with glossy brown stripes on the outer petals.

C. tomasinianus. Zones 3-8. This Crocus blooms a little

ahead of the preceding. The flowers are silvery on the outside, lavender inside.

Cyclamen atkinsii. Zones 6-10. We usually think of
Cyclamens as florist plants; but there are also several 8-in.
species which grow happily outdoors. *Atkinsii* is the earliest, blooming in February. Both white and pink varieties
are available. The foliage is marbled with silver. The plant
grows in the shade.

Eranthis hyemalis (Winter Aconite). Zones 3-9. The
Winter Aconites pop out of the snow in February like
little golden balls. They then open out like buttercups.
The plants are only about 4 in. tall and have a ruff of
finely-cut, green bracts at the base. They require light
shade.

Galanthus elwesii (Snowdrop). Zones 3-8. The Snowdrops often thrust up through the snow in late January,
but if it is very cold the flowers remain closed. When open,
they are small, pendent, bell-shaped blossoms with three
white, outer petals around an inner tube tipped with
green. The plants are about 1 ft. high. *Elwesii* is a particularly choice variety with much larger flowers than the
common variety, *nivalis.* Plant all Snowdrops in light
shade.

Hyacinthus azureus. Zones 6-8. This 5-in. Hyacinth has
upright clusters of small, true-blue, bell-like flowers in
March.

Iris bakeriana. Zones 7-10. This and the following bulbous Irises grow to about 6 in., but are something of a
nuisance because they should be dug up every spring after
they die down and stored until fall. *Bakeriana* has soft-blue
flowers blotched with deep purple. These appear in late
February or early March.

I. danfordiae. Zones 7-10. The canary-yellow flowers
tinged with green appear in February.

I. histrioides major. Zones 7-10. This is a very pretty, blue Iris with unusually large blossoms for such a small plant. They appear in late February or early March.

I. reticulata. Zones 7-10. The flowers of this Iris are a deep purple-blue with a bright yellow blotch on the lower petals; and to make them all the more attractive, they have a faint fragrance. Flowering starts in late February. Several good varieties are available.

Leucojum vernum (Snowflake). Zones 3-7. The Snowflake is very much like the Snowdrop. It grows in light shade; puts out drooping, bell-like, white flowers touched with green in March. It is about 1 ft. tall.

Narcissus asturiensis (often identified as *N. minimus*). Zones 3-10. This little trumpet Daffodil makes the following species look like a giant. It is only 3 in. tall, but you will be charmed by the gay, yellow trumpet flowers appearing in March.

N. cyclamineus. Zones 3-10. This Daffodil is 6 in. tall; has small trumpet flowers with wavy edges. They are a rich yellow and bloom in February or March. February Gold is an excellent variety, growing to about 12 in.

Scilla bifolia. Zones 5-10. This Scilla starts blooming right after the Winter Aconites in late February or early March. It is the earliest of its genus. The flowers are pendent and turquoise blue. The plant grows to about 8 in. It needs light shade.

S. sibirica (Siberian Squill). Zones 3-7. A March-bloomer, the Siberian Squill has three or four nodding, star-like bells on each 4-in. stem. They are bright blue, but a variety with white flowers can be had. The plant requires light shade.

S. tubergeniana. Zones 3-10. This Scilla is similar to the preceding, but blooms with *S. bifolia* in late February or early March. Its flowers are two shades of blue.

Tulipa kaufmanniana (Water Lily Tulip). Zones 3-8.

Whether these Tulips look more like six-pointed stars or Water Lilies is a matter for debate; but nobody can argue that they are not large and delightful. There are many varieties in various shades of red and yellow. They appear in March on upright stems, usually under 10 in. in length. The foliage is interestingly mottled, striped, or spotted.

T. pulchella violacea. Zones 3-8. A 4-in. Tulip blooming in March, this variety (sometimes called Violet Queen) has charming, little, red-purple flowers on slender stems.

Flowering shrubs. The best of these listed below are described in greater detail in the preceding chapter:

Arbutus unedo. Zones 7b-10. White flowers coinciding with red fruits.

Camellia japonica. Zones 7b-10. White, pink and red flowers.

C. sasanqua. Zones 7b-10. White and pink flowers.

Chimonanthus praecox. Zones 8-10. Pale yellow flowers.

Erica carnea. Zones 6-10. White to red flowers.

Hamamelis mollis. Zones 6-9. Yellow flowers.

Hamamelis vernalis. Zones 5-9. Yellow to reddish flowers.

Mahonia bealei. Zones 6b-10. Yellow flowers.

Most spectacular of the winter-flowering plants is the Common Camellia.

Two tiny flowers of the Wintersweet are barely open but perfume the air around them.

The oddly shaped little flowers of the Chinese Witchhazel open in midwinter.

This Vernal Witchhazel was photographed on the same freezing day as the Chinese species, but the flowers were closed.

Responding to the warmth of the sun and to that escaping through the foundation walls, Snowdrops bloom happily on a frigid early February day.

The Christmas Rose puts out its showy flowers even when snow piles up around it.

6

Green Grass in the Winter Garden

W HEN my sister-in-law, a California native who had never been out of the state, made her first trip East, it was December. I'll never forget her surprise when she looked out at the lawn the morning after her arrival. "Good grief!" she exclaimed. "Is that grass?"

I couldn't blame her for her dismay. Accustomed as I was to winter lawns in cold climates, I had to agree that the grass was a dismal sight. I could see a little green here and there, but mainly it was a tired, worn brown. Yet it happened to be a pretty good lawn!

Today, despite the fact that most northern and southern grasses go dormant in all areas except the warmest, there is absolutely no reason why winter lawns should not be a healthy, lovely green.

True enough, I am not at all certain that I want my *entire* lawn to be green. That would be too unnatural. I cannot reconcile in my mind a vast sweep of green grass when the rest of the garden is essentially gray and brown.

But to color a modest section of the lawn green—that's something else again. Try it in a walled courtyard; or in a sunny area surrounded by evergreens; or in any other small area that is somehow cut off so you can't see brown grass beyond (because the green next to the brown will just make the brown look worse). The prospect is delightful.

Dye it green

This is the simplest way to get a green lawn. All you have to do is mix a special color concentrate with water and spray it on the grass on a dry day with a garden sprayer. If you take pains to make a heavy application which completely covers all leaf blades, the color should last until spring. But if it doesn't, you can easily touch up worn spots as necessary. No matter how much of this special dye is applied, it will not harm the grass.

Owners of lawns planted to zoysia grass are particularly fond of the dye treatment because, although zoysia retains its dense, fine, springy texture throughout the winter, it turns the color of a camelhair coat. Other grasses can be dyed just as successfully, however.

Lawns in Zone 8

People living in the more humid parts of Zone 8 are lucky: They can have natural green lawns the year round. In actual fact, if they take the right steps, their lawns may be more beautiful in winter than in summer.

There are two ways to achieve this happy state of affairs.

1. The old way, which is slightly the more troublesome but gives better results, is to plant the lawn with Bermuda grass and to overseed it every fall with Annual or Perennial Rye grass. The overseeding is done in late September or

early October. Many people simply scatter the grass seed on top of the old lawn and keep it damp until germination occurs. But a better procedure (it is essential if you have much thatch in your lawn) is to mow the lawn as short as possible; remove the thatch by machine; then sow the seed at the rate of 5 to 20 lb. per 1000 sq. ft.; and water daily until germination occurs.

Studies made at the Mississippi Agricultural and Forestry Experiment Station indicate that Perennial Rye grass produces superior turf to Annual Rye. (The station used a variety named Medalist 11.) The lawn should be fertilized once every month during the winter with 2 lb. of ammonium nitrate or sewage sludge per 1000 sq. ft. The Rye grass fades out in late May or June.

2. The other way to have a year-round, green lawn is to sow it originally with Tall Fescue (Kentucky 31 or Alta). In Zone 8, this never goes into dormancy if you keep it watered and fertilized. However, it is a coarse grass with a tendency to become clumpy—especially if it is allowed to thin out. Autumn over-seeding with Tall Fescue is needed, therefore, to keep a dense, medium-textured stand.

Heat the lawn electrically

Although this may sound like a wild idea, a number of football fields are heated electrically in order to maintain a tough, green, springy turf late into the year. Golf greens have also been heated. So why shouldn't you be able to heat a small section of your lawn in the same way? You can.

Odd as it may seem, heating the lawn is more practical in cold climates than in warm. Less wattage is required; and northern grasses respond better than southern grasses. It follows that you should consider this idea only if you live in Zones 7 to 5. North of 5, winters are too severe.

Putting heat into the ground under grass accomplishes several things: It melts snow and ice as they land on the lawn; keeps the ground from freezing; dries the soil enough to let you walk on it without sinking in; permits you to reseed or resod the lawn at any time so that it need never look threadbare; and keeps the grass green.

Unfortunately, the greenness of the grass depends on the variety used. Blades of Bluegrass and Fescue stay green at the bottom, but the tips turn brown in very cold weather because they are too high above the ground to be protected by the heat. On the other hand, Perennial Rye grass retains its green color well because it is a hardier species. And Bent Grass retains its color because it is low-growing.

The heating cables used in lawns are the same as those used in hotbeds and driveways. They are installed 6 in. deep in narrow cuts made with a spade, and they are spaced 1 ft. apart. The system should be designed to provide 10 watts per square foot. Controlled by a thermostat, the system goes on and off when the sun is shining or the air temperature is high; stays on almost continuously during cloudy days and nights in cold weather.

The cost of installation totals about $100 for a 400-sq.-ft. lawn. If you have a 2-cents-per-kilowatt-hour electric rate, the cost of operation averages approximately a dollar a day.

Synthetic turf

By the end of 1971, roughly two-dozen home owners in the Miami area had converted their lawns to synthetic grass; and one of the distributors of this material told me that he expected sales to other home owners to boom in the years ahead.

The Miamians' interest in synthetic turf stems from the

problems many of them have had in recent years in maintaining natural turf. The desire for a green lawn in winter is not a factor because the various grasses grown in the area stay green the year round. But the mere fact that Miamians are putting in synthetic lawns indicates that this is a practical idea for home owners throughout the country.

Actually, since the problems of lawn maintenance are universal, Northerners in all climate zones have even more reason to put in synthetic turf than Southerners: It is a good way to have an outdoor patch of green when the mercury plummets to zero and below.

Two types of synthetic turf are sold for home use.

1. One designed strictly for light traffic areas—not for recreational areas—is made of *polyethylene*. Its strap-like, inch-long blades do not look very natural close-up; they make a crunching sound underfoot; and they are not pleasant to walk on in bare feet (which children might want to do in the summer). But these are not serious disadvantages since the turf is meant mainly to be looked at from a distance.

An important advantage which this turf enjoys is its permeable backing: If you lay it on compacted gravel or soil which has been stripped of sod, water and oxygen will work down through it to the tree roots underlying the lawn.

Polyethylene turf comes in 3-ft.-wide rolls. Each strip must be laid in the same direction to avoid obvious differences in the grain. Before the rolls are laid, the base should be treated with a soil sterilant to prevent possible weed growth. It should then be rolled perfectly smooth. The strips are easily anchored with metal hooks driven into the soil.

2. The other type of synthetic turf is made of *nylon* with very dense, short, soft blades resembling those of Bent Grass or fine Bermuda Grass. This is much more

durable than polyethylene turf (it is similar to the turf in football stadiums) and is meant for use in recreational areas. But unfortunately, the grass has an impermeable backing; it should not be installed near trees, shrubs, and vines because it would not permit water and air to reach the roots.

In actual practice, nylon turf, which comes in long rolls up to 15 ft. wide, is laid over a base of concrete, asphalt, wood or brick. As in the case of polyethylene turf, each strip must be laid in the same direction. The base must be perfectly smooth and sloped to one or more sides to allow water to drain off. The turf is simply rolled out over the base like a carpet, or it is anchored with double-faced tape. If a very resilient surface is required, a plastic, shock-absorbing pad is laid between the base and the turf.

3. Once down, both the polyethylene and nylon turfs require little maintenance. They can be cleaned, when dry, with a vacuum cleaner; washed with a hose under pressure. Stains are removed with detergents. Damaged spots can be cut out and filled with a plug of new turf. Snow is removed with a shovel, plow, broom or blower. The grass will not fade, mildew or decay. It has considerable resistance to flame and is non-allergenic.

The worst drawback of synthetic turf, of course, is that it does not look quite right. Its other major drawback is its determination to expand in hot weather. This causes joints between strips to pucker slightly unless an expansion gap—which isn't attractive in winter—is left between the strips. The effect is particularly noticeable on nylon turf.

7

Birds and Squirrels in the Winter Garden

ONE of the most entrancing features of the winter garden is the wildlife which occupies it. I enjoy wildlife in the summer garden, too; but despite the fact that it is more colorful and vocal at that time, it doesn't capture my attention so fully. In winter, there is less foliage to hide it; there are few flowers or fragrances to give it competition.

Further than that, because cold weather threatens the survival of birds, they become more dependent on me and dare to come up so close that I can enjoy their every movement without aid of binoculars. Just this noon, for example, my wife and I tarried over our usually hasty lunch to watch a chickadee on the feeder outside the kitchen window. She was a funny little thing, picking out seeds as fast as she could move and deliberately spitting them over the feeder rim on to the ground until finally she had unearthed a sunflower seed of her choice. Then she darted away in the chickadee's typical, roller-coaster flight, only to dart in from another direction a minute later. In the gray of a winter day, she was a spot of brightness which transformed the entire garden area within view; and we recognized once again the value of catering to her and all her friends when fall begins to slip into winter.

BIRDS IN YOUR WINTER GARDEN

To attract birds, there are three things you should give them:

Water for birds

Birds need water to drink and to bathe in as much in winter as in warm weather; but when natural water sources are frozen over, it is hard for them to satisfy their needs unless you lend a helping hand. A shallow bird bath situated out of the easy reach of cats, and within view of the house (so you can enjoy the action), is called for.

To keep the water from freezing, place in the bottom of the basin a small immersion heater like that used in aquariums or poultry houses. I confess that I have not made a study of what wattage is required to cope with low temperatures in all parts of the country. But looking back to the days when I raised chickens, I can vouch for the fact that a 150-watt poultry heater does a splendid job down to ten below (the coldest we ever got), and undoubtedly would have been satisfactory at much lower readings. In warmer regions, a 75-watt heater should be ample.

Shelter for birds

Shelter for birds means three things: Dense trees or shrubs in which they can take refuge from winter storms; houses in which birds that normally nest in tree holes can sleep; and roosting boxes in which many types of birds can gather at night to keep warm.

Selecting plants to give shelter against storms does not call for unusual head-scratching. Some of the most beautiful plants used to ornament the garden are also outstanding in the shelter department. These are the needled evergreens—and most especially the dense Firs, Cedars, False Cypresses, Spruces, Yews and Hemlocks. Failing to use these, you may resort to any other large plant—evergreen or deciduous—which has sufficiently dense branches and/or leaves to break the wind and ward off ice and snow. (In my own garden, when storms rage, I suspect that as many birds are to be found in the tangle of Forsythia and Beauty Bush that divides me from my nearest neighbor as in the numerous conifers which grace the place.)

Birdhouses for hole-nesting birds are available in profusion from many stores; but it doesn't take much skill or effort to make your own out of ¾-in. lumber or exterior-grade plywood. The design can be as fancy as you like; but a cube with a top sloping from the back down to the front, like a shed roof, is the easiest to make and pleasing to both birds and the human eye. The dimensions required for a selected assortment of birds are given in the table. If you stick to these, the birds will flock to your garden; if you deviate, they will go next door. Three other things you must do to keep birds happy are (1) to make the roof or a side panel removable so you can clean the house occasionally, (2) to drill two ¼-in. holes in the bottom to drain off water which may get in, and (3) to drill two or three ¼-in. holes in the front or side panels just under the roof to provide air circulation in hot weather.

When putting up a birdhouse, use screws so that you can easily take it down if the location does not prove attractive. The house can be attached to a tree, but there is some evidence that birds consider houses mounted on posts to be safer from cats. If you cater to this whim, go

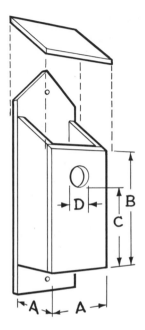

one step farther and surround the post with a wide strip of metal to stop climbing felines from reaching the top.

Since birds are not always overjoyed with near feathered neighbors, it is advisable to space houses at least 25 to 30 ft. apart. Face the entrance holes away from the pre-vailing wind. Avoid locations in dense shade; however, chickadees, nuthatches, titmouses and downy woodpeckers like to be close to groves of trees and in partial shade. Most birds, especially bluebirds, seem to prefer homes facing an open field or lawn. Purple martins go even fur-ther and demand that their homes be located in the middle of an open area.

In the winter, when temperatures drop, birdhouses are often crowded not only with their regular occupants, but

Dimensions for Birdhouses [a]

(See illustration on page 196 for corresponding lettered parts.)

Kind of Bird	A Size of Floor (inches)	B Depth of Bird Box (inches)	C Height of Entrance Above Floor (inches)	D Diameter of Entrance Hole (inches)	Height to Fasten Above Ground (feet)
Bluebird	5×5	8	6	1½	5–10
Chickadee	4×4	8–10	6–8	1⅛	6–15
Titmouse	4×4	8–10	6–8	1¼	6–15
Nuthatch	4×4	8–10	6–8	1¼	12–20
House wren and Bewick's wren	4×4	6–8	4–6	1–1¼	6–10
Carolina wren	4×4	6–8	4–6	1½	6–10
Violet-green swallow and Tree swallow	5×5	6	1–5	1½	10–15
Purple martin [b]	6×6	6	1	2½	15–20
House finch	6×6	6	4	2	8–12
Starling	6×6	16–18	14–16	2	10–25
Crested flycatcher	6×6	8–10	6–8	2	8–20
Flicker	7×7	16–18	14–16	2½	6–20
Golden-fronted woodpecker and red-headed woodpecker	6×6	12–15	9–12	2	12–20
Downy woodpecker	4×4	8–10	6–8	1¼	6–20
Hairy woodpecker	6×6	12–15	9–12	1½	12–20
Screech owl	8×8	12–15	9–12	3	10–30
Saw-whet owl	6×6	10–12	8–10	2½	12–20
Barn owl	10×18	15–18	4	6	12–18
Sparrow hawk	8×8	12–15	9–12	3	10–30
Wood duck	10×18	10–24	12–16	4	10–20

[a] Taken from "Homes for Birds," Conservation Bulletin 14, U.S. Department of the Interior.

[b] These are dimensions for a house for one pair of birds. Usually martin houses are built with apartments for eight or more pairs of birds.

also with as many of their friends as can squeeze in to get warm. Some of these are hole-nesting birds; others build nests in the open. To accommodate what may sometimes become an overflow crowd, build large roosting boxes. These are designed like a shed-roof birdhouse, but are about a foot square and 2 to 3 ft. high. The entrance hole is 3 in. across and located 1 to 2 ins. above the floor of the box—rather than near the top—so that the air heated by the birds' bodies will not escape. Glue short lengths of ¼-in. dowel into the sides of the box for the birds to roost on. The dowels should be staggered irregularly so that one bird will not be right above another. Install the roosting box in a well sheltered place about 10 ft. above the ground and facing South.

Food for birds

I refuse to get caught up in the debate between those who say we are spoiling the birds and making them lazy by starting to feed them too early in the fall, and those who say that birds should be fed the year round. There is merit in both positions. But it is obvious that if you want birds to brighten your winter garden, you can hardly feed them too much or too frequently.

To be sure, you may refuse to feed them during warm weather. But don't be too slow about setting out your feeders, suet boxes, and grit boxes when September rolls around. With plenty of natural food still available, the birds may not take immediate full advantage of your handouts; but they will at least discover what is available, and will be ready to partake when chill weather wipes out the insects and summer fruits.

If you hand-feed birds enough, there is no doubt that a number of species will be able to live happily through the winter on that alone. But what about those who prefer

For the Schulers in winter 1972 the sudden arrival of a flock of evening grosbeaks added new color and excitement to our garden.

fleshy fruits to seeds? And what of the cost of providing so much food? And what happens if you take a winter vacation in the South Seas? And to give the go-easy-on-feeding-birds advocates their due—is it really smart to reduce the self-sufficiency of birds?

No. If you are going to persuade lots of birds to make your garden their winter abode, you should see to it that the garden contains plants which the birds can feed on in winter. Fortunately, there are many of these; and to make matters even better, a sizable percentage of them have such ornamental value that you would plant them even if you had no interest in birds.

TREES AND SHRUBS THAT WINTER BIRDS FEED ON

Plants are listed in descending order of importance; but even those listed last attract birds.

Plants marked ** have high ornamental value and are described in Chapters 3 and 4. Plants marked * are effective as ornamentals but are not described.

North: New England states, Delaware, Indiana, Kentucky, Maryland, Michigan, Minnesota, New Jersey, New York, Ohio, Pennsylvania, Virginia, West Virginia, Wisconsin
> *Pinus banksiana, P. thunbergii**, P. koraiensis**, P. resinosa**, P. rigida, P. strobus***
> *Quercus alba**, Q. coccinea**, Q. macrocarpa*, Q. montana, Q. palustris**, Q. rubra***
> *Juniperus virginiana***
> *Acer ginnala*, A. negundo, A. rubra, A. saccharum***
> *Picea species***
> *Fagus species***
> *Betula papyrifera**, B. populifolia*
> *Liriodendron tulipifera***

Tsuga species**
Alnus species
Carya species**
Fraxinus species
Abies species**
*Ilex glabra, I. opaca***, *I. pedunculosa***, *I. verticillata***
*Crataegus crus-galli, C. lavallei, C. phaenopyrum***

South: *Alabama, Arkansas, Florida, Georgia, Louisiana, Mississippi, North Carolina, southeastern Oklahoma, South Carolina, Tennessee, eastern Texas*
    *Pinus caribaea, P. echinata, P. palustris***, *P. taeda*
    *Quercus laurifolia, Q. marilandica, Q. nigra, Q. phellos**,*
      *Q. virginiana***
    *Ilex cassine, I. decidua, I. opaca***, *I. verticillata***,
      *I. vomitoria***
    *Myrica cerifera, M. pensylvanica**, M. pumila*
    Nyssa species**
    Fagus species**
    *Juniperus virginiana***
    Acer species**
    *Liriodendron tulipifera***
    Carya species**
    Celtis species

Plains States: *Eastern Colorado, Illinois, Iowa, Kansas, eastern Montana, Missouri, Nebraska, North Dakota, northwestern Oklahoma, South Dakota, central Texas, eastern Wyoming*
    Celtis occidentalis, C. laevigata
    *Ilex decidua, I. glabra, I. pedunculosa***, *I. verticillata***
    Alnus species
    *Pinus contorta**, P. latifolia, P. flexilis**, P. ponderosa***
    *Quercus imbricaria***, *Q. macrocarpa, Q. marilandica,*
      Q. stellata

Juniperus horizontalis**, J. scopulorum**, J. virgini-ana**

Mountain States: *Arizona, western Colorado, Idaho, west-ern Montana, Nevada, New Mexico, eastern Oregon, west-ern Texas, Utah, eastern Washington, western Wyoming*
Pinus cembroides, P. flexilis*, P. contorta*, P. pon-derosa**
Celtis douglasii, C. occidentalis, C. reticulata
Juniperus monosperma, J. occidentalis**, J. scopulo-rum**, J. utahensis
Quercus chrysolepis**, Q. emoryi, Q. gambelii, Q. grisea, Q. utahensis
Arctostaphylos uva-ursi**
Abies concolor**, A. lasiocarpa
Picea engelmannii**, P. glauca**, P. pungens

Far West: *California, western Oregon, western Washington*
Pinus contorta*, P. coulteri**, P. jeffreyi, P. lamberti-ana*, P. monticola**, P. ponderosa**
Quercus chrysolepis**, Q. douglasii, Q. garryana*, Q. kellogii*, Q. lobata**
Alnus species
Juniperus californica, J. occidentalis*, J. scopulorum**
Arctostaphylos uva-ursi**
Arbutus menziesii**
Abies concolor**, A. grandis, A. lasiocarpa, A. mag-nifica*, A. nobilis*
Picea engelmannii**, P. glauca albertiana, P. sitchensis*

SQUIRRELS IN THE GARDEN

To listen to bird-lovers talk, you might think they hated squirrels; but I can't make myself believe they really do.

True, squirrels that continually get into your bird feeders
are a pest. But can anyone close his eyes to a pair of
squirrels skipping through the tree tops, rising on their
haunches to eat maple seeds, or taunting your dogs?

To me, the big, fat, bushy gray and black squirrels are
as attractive as any bird, and many times more comical
and ingratiating. Only a month ago I watched a gray
squirrel and a little red squirrel (a species I dislike because they are so unfriendly) playing tag across the front
lawn. The red squirrel in the lead was running for all he
was worth; the gray came loping along behind, moving
just fast enough to spur the red on, but not fast enough
to catch him. It was a sight I had never seen before, and
I loved every minute of it.

And then, just two days ago, a gray squirrel managed
to shinny up the pole into the bird feeder in front of the
kitchen window. He looked at my wife and me through
the window; flipped his tail in disdain; turned his back,
and gobbled to heart's content. Rapping on the window
disturbed him not at all. He was a picture of mischievous
calm—a charmer from the tips of his tiny ears to the end
of his fat tail.

Squirrels are not difficult to please and to keep more or
less under control if you have trees to provide food and
give protection against dogs and cats. Hickories and Pecans
are favorite food trees, and when these are pretty well
stripped, the White Oaks with their sweet acorns followed
by the Red Oaks with their bitter acorns attract the squirrels' attention. Since there are more Oaks than Hickories,
acorns are actually the staple diet of the squirrels. Wildlife studies show that a single squirrel gathers—or would
like to gather—7 lb. of acorns a day. Other nuts which
squirrels relish are black walnuts, hazelnuts and chestnuts.
I have also noted that they like the seeds in the winged
fruits of Norway Maples. This is a happy circumstance

because, unless eaten, the seeds germinate and put up hundreds of little trees every spring—usually in places where you don't want them.

Even if you have plenty of nut trees, however, squirrels will often show an interest in the seed you put out for birds. So it is necessary to take steps to keep them from getting into your feeders. This is best done by placing the feeder on a smooth metal post about 5 ft. off the ground in the middle of an open area, 10 ft. from the nearest tree limb or comparable perch. As long as the surface of the post is slick, a squirrel cannot climb it; but when it becomes rusty, you should coat it regularly with axle grease. The alternative is to surround the post just below the feeder with a 15- to 18-in.-wide metal cone hung open end down.

Feeders mounted on wood posts must be protected by metal cones; and this is also true of those which are hung on wires from tree limbs. In the latter case, of course, the cone (also hung open end down) goes above the feeder so that a squirrel sliding down the wire, or leaping from the limb, will be stopped by it and shaken from it when it wobbles under his weight.

To keep squirrels from setting up housekeeping in bird-houses, simply tack a metal sheet around the entrance holes. This will keep them from gnawing the holes open far enough to let them in.

8

Garden Structures and
Furnishings for Winter Beauty

As I said in Chapter 2, the attractive winter garden is largely a garden of form. And there are few shapes which do more for the garden than those created by man out of masonry and other non-plant materials.

The North Carolina garden shown on the next few pages is an outstanding example of this. I saw it first on a brilliant spring day when it was splashed with colorful Azaleas and Dogwoods; and yet even then I was captured by its delicate-ranging-to-simple form. When I visited the garden a second time—in winter—its form was more pronounced and lovelier than ever.

The gazebo in the middle of the tall pines is exquisite. The little round pool with a figure of Pan and the urchin crouched on the wall are captivating. But the high point of the entire garden is the walled area deliberately created for viewing from inside the house. The white brick wall separating the area from the woodland beyond is shaped like a graceful J. I may seem to be stretching a point, but

In the spring this gazebo is given some competition for at-
tention by Azaleas and Dogwoods. But in the winter it is the
focal point of the woodland area.

This North Carolina garden might be called a modern version of the form-filled Williamsburg garden pictured on preceding pages.

I think that if the area within the J were planted to nothing but grass, the effect would still be a delight, such is the simple beauty of the wall. But Stanley Underhill, the Boston landscape architect who designed the garden, went one step further and used the wall as a backdrop for shrubs and trees. The most important of these are three large circles of sheared Japanese Holly which are enclosed within a low ring of Holly. Mr. Underhill's inspiration for this unusual arrangement was a piece of Korean sculpture—itself a ring—which he featured quietly with the Hollies.

WALLS

From the time man first started to garden until the 16th century and even later, most gardens were walled. In early history, the primary purpose of the walls was to provide protection against enemies; but they also were for shelter against wind and dust. Today in the United States, gardens completely surrounded by walls are rare, except in California. But walls in various parts of the garden are extremely common. These serve many practical purposes: To retain the soil and provide level land on hillside lots; to give privacy; to protect against the wind; to keep out people and animals; and so on. But while home owners may not think much about it, walls also serve an important aesthetic purpose: They give gardens form.

Walls give form to a garden

Walls give form to the garden because they are crisp and rigid in a setting which is anything but crisp and rigid. Looking at a wall in a garden, you instantly recognize its shape no matter how much of it you can see. By contrast, while many plants have distinct shapes when silhouetted against a solid background, their shapes become indistinct when they are mixed in with other plants.

Similarly, walls give form to the garden because they stand out as such definite, precise lines that there is no doubt in the mind about the shape of the area they bound. On the other hand, plants cannot delineate the shape of an area so clearly because the foliage, twigs, and branches make blurred, imprecise lines.

Finally, by serving as a background for plants, walls give form to the garden by highlighting the shape of the plants. For instance, an espalier in front of a wall is a distinct shape. But take the wall away, and the espalier loses all value as a form.

In short, if you are trying to give your garden form, you should consider the use of walls almost before anything else.

How you use them, of course, depends on many things: The size and shape of the garden; the contours of the land; the view; the positions of large trees and shrubs; the proximity to neighboring houses or gardens; and so on. You certainly cannot arbitrarily build walls just to give your garden form in winter. On the contrary, you must study their possible use and placement with utmost care; and you must do this while standing in the garden, and also while looking out at it from inside the house.

Types of wall

The type of wall you build also requires study, though the answer is not so hard to come by. The following are points to be considered:

Which wall material will blend best with the house? This doesn't mean the garden wall must exactly match the house walls. But as a rule, if the house is, say, brick, the garden walls should also be brick. This is particularly true if the walls connect with or come close to the house.

Will any of the walls be retaining walls? The pressure which retaining walls must withstand varies with the condition of the soil, the amount of ground water and the height of the walls. Generally, retaining walls under about 3 ft. high can be constructed like free-standing walls. Higher retaining walls, however, must usually be much stronger and more massive than free-standing walls; and this, in turn, usually means that they are built of poured concrete.

What will the walls cost? All masonry walls are expensive and this is probably the main reason why fences outnumber them. But it is a mistake to assume that one masonry wall costs the same as another, because there are actually big differences between them.

Finally, you must consider the appearance of the walls.

Poured concrete walls, or masonry walls covered with cement plaster, are the most uncompromisingly stiff, severe, and stark. They have no softness whatever because they have no texture. But if you want to bring out the form and texture of plants in complete detail, concrete and plaster walls are unrivaled. Since poured reinforced concrete also has much greater strength than other types of masonry, it is also used when you must build walls of unusual height.

Concrete blocks are used in more walls today than any other material because they are easy and comparatively inexpensive to lay up. The appearance of the finished walls depends on the texture of the blocks, the bond (the pattern in which the blocks are laid), and the skill with which the joints are tooled. Great variation is possible because the blocks are made in numerous sizes and textures; and there are a number of bonds. (To my mind, the stacked bond is one of the best. In this, the blocks are laid up one directly over the other so that you wind up with a wall with strong vertical and horizontal lines.) As a rule, all concrete block walls look best when painted, although some blocks are made with integral color.

Unfortunately, despite the many possibilities that concrete blocks offer, I don't think I have ever seen a wall I could call handsome. But many are better than passable.

Pierced walls made with sculptured concrete blocks are another matter. These are high ornamental screens through which you can see from one part of the garden to another; and they are useful if you want to define the boundaries of a garden area, but don't want to cut off completely the view of the garden beyond. They are also fairly good as wind screens, because they break up and filter the winds (see Chapter 5). However, the walls have so much texture that they compete for interest with the plants in a garden; and they are of little value as a background for plants.

Stone walls, whether laid up dry or with mortar, are the most beautiful of all garden walls *if* they are well built. I emphasize the "if" because the art of building with stone—and it is an art—has just about disappeared. But maybe you will be lucky enough to find an old-timer who is still active.

The beauty of a stone wall lies in its rough texture, color, and tapestry-like effect. But it is a quiet, unassuming kind of wall which blends into the garden because it is made of natural materials. Consequently, it does not have such prominent form as other walls; and it does not bring out the form of plants set in front of it.

Brick walls, if not painted, have the same deficiencies (if you want to call them deficiencies). But their beauty rivals that of stone walls, especially after weathering for a few years. Coated with white paint, however, a brick wall is in a class by itself in winter gardens which are not snow-covered from fall till spring. It has a gentle texture which gives it a unity with plants that is unattainable with a poured concrete or plastered wall. Yet it has strong lines and a distinct form; and because it is made of many small, even-sized pieces, it has an over-all smoothness that does not interfere with the appearance of plants placed in front of it.

(No matter what a wall is made of, its *color* is something to weigh carefully. A white wall, as I just indicated, is not good in regions with a great deal of snow because it becomes lost in the background. This can be corrected to some extent, however, by giving it a dark-colored cap and/or by using it as a background for a lot of plants. By contrast, a dark-colored wall stands out strongly in snow country, but becomes indistinct and sometimes almost invisible in warmer climates unless it is silhouetted against a lawn, water or the sky. If you are looking for a compromise, a light- to medium-colored wall, such as pale-pink brick, is the obvious choice.)

FENCES

The ability of fences to give form to the winter garden varies greatly. Like walls, all wood and ornamental iron fences give definition to the area they bound. But since fences are essentially two-dimensional, they themselves have little form. They have a pattern or tracery which has undeniable merit in the winter garden and adds to the garden's interest; but they lack the three-dimensional substance of a wall.

Finally, there is only one type of fence which serves as a good background for plants. That is one made of wide, vertical, rough-sawn boards nailed edge to edge. To look well, this must be about 5 ft. high or higher; and while it may be painted white, silvery gray or some other light

color, it is most effective when allowed to weather naturally or when treated with a bleaching oil or light-colored
transparent oil stain.

Tall, stockade fences made of debarked cedar saplings
also serve as a background for plants, but less successfully
because they themselves have so much texture. When my
wife and I bought our Lyme home, we found a small section of stockade fencing made of sawn saplings; but it
struck us as being so ineffective and downright dreary that
we were on the verge of knocking it down until she suggested painting it white. The transformation was astound-
ing; but the fence still isn't anything to exclaim about.

My fence's lack of beauty brings up a point which,
although not entirely germane to this chapter, is worth
consideration whenever you build a fence: If it isn't
designed skillfully, it will detract more than it will add
to the charm of the winter garden. This is because it is so
prominent in a garden which Nature has stripped of
foliage.

Sad to say, pretty fences and handsome fences are a
rarity today. One reason for this is that many fences are of
skimpy dimensions. The prefabricated pickets sold by
many lumber yards are an example. They are just skinny
—a pale shadow of the pickets our grandfathers used.
Another reason for our sad fences is that they are not
properly maintained once erected. All fences demand
maintenance, but some more than others. If they don't
receive it, they begin to fall apart in short order. There are
few things which look as rundown as a fence with peeling
paint, flapping pickets and reeling posts and rails.

The third reason for my unhappiness with today's fences
is that a lot of modern designs are without grace and
sometimes border on ugliness. Fences with interwoven
boards are an example. Even louvered fences, simple as
they are, have little eye appeal.

GAZEBOS

The gazebo is about as useless a garden furnishing as I can think of; but useless or not, it is one of the most charming. Ever since I first saw the gazebo pictured on page 206, I have had an absolute passion for all of them. To be sure, that one is exceptionally lovely. Others are much simpler and plainer. But there must be something about all gazebos which brings out the best in their designers.

Gazebos are of ornamental value in the garden the whole year round. I doubt that they contribute more in one season than another. But simply because there are fewer leaves to hide them, they are most prominent in winter and consequently the impact of their form on the garden is greatest in that season.

SCULPTURE

As in almost every other garden book I have written, I must preface this section with the statement that garden sculpture does not include gazing balls, plastic ducks, fawns, black-sambo hitching posts, and all the other frightful junk sold along highways as garden ornaments. There is no place in the garden for such stuff. It's an insult to passersby on the street, to your neighbors, and most of all to yourself.

Garden sculpture—which should more properly be called "sculpture which is displayed in the garden," because much of it might just as well be displayed indoors— must have some artistic merit. It need not be the work of a Moore, Lipchitz or Rodin. It matters not whether it is made of marble, granite, bronze, lead, iron, steel, wood, plastics or weather-resistant ceramics. It may include sundials, birdbaths, fountains—even garden benches—as well as figures. The only thing that counts is that it is a work of art—major or minor but, in every case, capable of evoking an emotional response from the viewer.

If you have plenty of money, there is no problem about finding or commissioning really good sculpture for your garden. But if your income is modest, you must search hard to come up with something which is a little better than run-of-the-mill. The basic difficulty here is that, at some time in history, some one decided that garden sculpture is different from other sculpture; and as a result, the only pieces available from the studios that specialize in garden sculpture are overly ornate, pretentious throwbacks to the Italian Renaissance and Victorian eras. These are suitable for castles, but not for American gardens of the 1970s. As I just said, however, if you hunt, you can probably unearth something that pleases eye and soul. We found a charming little ceramic St. Francis birdbath for under $20, and grew to like it so much that we have given copies to four or five friends. One of our daughters found a sundial cast out of aluminum on a semi-mass-production basis which is no masterpiece, but for $8 makes a pleasing ornament on a garden wall. And just a year ago, at a craft fair, we ran across some figures made, of all things, out of the steel parts of old farm tools. They had surprising distinction, and sold for only $40 up.

Except for collectors, most people buying sculpture for their gardens buy only a few pieces—each one for a specific location; but occasionally they buy a piece because they like it and then figure out where to put it. In either case, there are no rules you must follow in displaying the sculpture. I have been in gardens in which a single piece is the focal point of the entire garden, in others in which the pieces are tucked in among the plants so you come on them unexpectedly, and in still others in which the balance between sculpture and plants is about 50-50. All methods of display are effective.

When you are designing a garden for winter as well as summer enjoyment, however, you must make sure that your sculpture is prominent in the winter garden; otherwise it fails in its purpose of giving form to the garden in winter.

Obviously, if the sculpture is prominent in the summer garden, it is going to be at least equally prominent in the winter garden. But if the sculpture is played down in the summer garden (a practice I happen to favor), it may not stand out in the winter garden either; all depends on whether the plants around the piece are evergreen or deciduous.

The appearance of snow and ice on the sculpture should also be considered. Under snow, some pieces become lumpish; others gain interest. Similarly, some pieces acquire an interesting glaze of ice; others drip with icicles which destroy their shapes. Unfortunately, it is impossible to predict how a given piece of sculpture will react; so when you place it in the garden for the first time, you must take your chances. But once you have actually seen it laden with snow or ice, you may find a change of location advisable in order to protect it as much as possible or, vice versa, to expose it to even more snow and ice.

DRIFTWOOD

Under the heading of driftwood, I include any dead tree or tree-part of picturesque shape and attractive color.

Offhand, I can think of only one garden in which I have seen a large piece of driftwood used for ornament; but it is in southern California and therefore does not qualify for illustration in this book. Silhouetted against a high brick wall, it is, however, a compelling object. In a winter setting, it would be even more so if it were placed well away from deciduous trees and shrubs which would detract from its uniqueness.

STONES

In the American garden, stones will never be given the importance they are given in the Japanese garden. This is no cause for regret. But it is regrettable that more American gardeners do not recognize the contribution which a handsome boulder or rock outcropping makes to the garden. I hesitate to say that this contribution is greater in winter than summer, because in warm weather stones not only have great beauty in themselves, but are also superb foils for plants. But like sculpture and walls, stones in winter add form to the garden. Under a mantle of snow they are mysterious mounds. Then, when the snow melts from them (long before it melts off the surrounding ground), they appear in striking gray relief against the white background.

Outcroppings are particularly effective, and it is a lucky gardener who has one. Even so, most lucky gardeners fail to take full advantage of them. The secret is very simple. Scrape as much soil as you can from the rock and from inside the fissures; then remove the rest with a high-pressure hose. At first the result seems unnatural. But then you begin to discover the full beauty of the rock—its color, texture, striations, seams and, most of all, its form.

Placing large stones in the garden to create an effect, or an actual picture, is more difficult than handling outcrops. There is a temptation to make arrangements of stones just as garden-club ladies make arrangements of flowers. But this almost always ends in disastrous artificiality because we don't have Japanese sensitivity toward stones, and we rarely take the time to study how stones are arranged by Nature. It is much better, therefore, to give each interesting stone you find individual treatment.

In my book *Gardening with Ease* I give a number of suggestions for placing stones in the garden; and since I cannot improve on them, I repeat them here:

1. ·Stones are made to order for those spots in the garden where lack of sun, poor soil, bad drainage, and so on, make it difficult to grow plants. Needless to say, however, you should not use them in such locations unless they improve the appearance of the areas and are, in turn, complimented by the areas.

2. Since stones weigh too much to permit you to experiment very much with their placement, one of the first things you should decide is whether to use a stone as a prominent feature (like a statue), or as a subtle element designed to surprise and delight the visitor. Stones that fall into the first category need to have plenty of space around them, and should be set against a contrasting backdrop. (They are especially effective when placed on an open paved or graveled surface. And they would be equally effective on grass—if you could figure out some way to avoid trimming the grass around them.)

Stones that play a subtle role in the garden can be tucked away almost anywhere, but should not be so hidden that visitors might trip over them.

3. Stones usually look attractive in front of walls made of brick, concrete block, vertical boards, and plywood, but not in front of shingled or clapboard walls.

4. Because they are natural objects, stones should be placed where you would find them in nature—on the ground. This does not mean that they must always be at your feet, of course. They can be at eye level or even higher, if they are on a hillside. But they should not be

raised by artificial means. They should neither sit atop tree stumps or pedestals, nor be placed in an obviously precarious position from which logic tells you that they would fall if someone had not indulged in a little trickery with mirrors.

5. It is important, too, that a stone be set in a vertical or horizontal position according to its placement in nature. For a slab of limestone to be set on end, for example, would not only be unnatural but would make it look like a tombstone. By the same token, it would be wrong to lay a spire of sandstone from a desert canyon flat.

6. The textured quality of a stone is enhanced when it is in sunlight or light shadow. It suffers when it is in mottled sun and shade. And in deep shade it looks like nothing at all.

7. Some types of stone are great collectors of lichens, which add immeasurably to their beauty. The conglomerate rocks found in the Shawangunk Mountains of New York State, for example, are noted for their coverings of these strange little plants. If you can find handsome samples of similar, lichen-covered stones, grab them quickly. If you can't, look for stones with a rather rough surface and place them in an exposed part of the garden where they will be struck by the winds that carry lichens across the country.

Designed by Thomas Church of San Francisco, this Maryland garden is really nothing more than a slightly sloping lawn which is given handsome definition by the low, white brick walls surrounding it. Opening off the house, a long flagstone terrace with ever-so-straight lines flows into a circular terrace which projects into a corner of the lawn. A Japanese Maple is planted in a raised bed on the long terrace.

*Few if any private gardens in the United States boast such an
array of sculpture as the one shown here and on the following
four pages. But even if you cannot hope to own a Henry
Moore, Lipchitz or Lachaise, study of the pictures (1) shows
the contribution that sculpture can make to the winter garden
and (2) gives some valuable lessons in how to place sculpture
in relation to plants and how to mount individual pieces for
maximum effect.*

Mobile by David Burt gains prominence in the bleak winter garden and, in turn, adds interest to the garden. (Piece from the Sculpture Center, New York City.)

Two obvious reasons that you should take full advantage of rock outcroppings or boulders if you are lucky enough to have them in your garden. The huge rock in a vast Rhododendron garden (below) was scrubbed clean with high-pressure hoses. Pachysandra has been encouraged to grow in the main fissures of the rock (above).

9

The Winter Garden at Night

THE winter garden reaches a crescendo of beauty on cold, clear nights when the moon is full and tree limbs make jagged shadows on a lawn mantled with unspoiled snow. But unhappily, there are only a few nights in any year when this picture can be seen. Unhappily, too, man cannot duplicate it with electric lights. It is possible, however, to use lights to create striking beauty in the garden.

One of the most entrancing garden scenes I can recall was the product of my Cousin Harry's installation of three or four outdoor floodlights.

The living and dining rooms in Harry's modern house are walled on one side with glass to admit the view of a granite cliff just across the terrace. As cliffs go, this one isn't very large or spectacular; but it is attractively rugged. The granite drops in a precipitous, fissured mass for several feet; then breaks up into boulders interspersed with trees, well-chosen evergreen shrubs, and a tiny pool. By day, the cliff is pleasantly gray and green; on dry nights, under Harry's floodlights, it becomes gray and black—full of shadows and mystery. When it rains, the rocks glisten and turn phosphorescent green where the lichens cling. And when snow falls, the cliff becomes a masterpiece by Claude Monet.

On the evening I recall especially, Harry and Dolly were having a party. It began to snow softly. Suddenly, through the flakes, a tiny screech owl dropped down on the far edge of the terrace at the base of the cliff and began to hop around. The party came to a mesmerized halt which lasted until the bird finally flew away.

Few gardens, alas, are blessed with cliffs. But as long as they have trees and shrubs, they can be turned into a minor fairyland with a few lights; and, what most people fail to realize is that this can be just as entrancing on winter nights as on summer nights.

Equipment needed

Your garden can be wired for a temporary or permanent lighting installation. Until you know exactly where and how lights should be placed, you must use temporary wiring only. If you strive for different lighting effects in winter and summer, you may find it advisable to use temporary wiring at all times. Permanent wiring is better, however, because it is buried in the ground where it cannot be seen and is safe from damage.

However you wire the garden, all equipment used must be weatherproof—designed specifically for outdoor installation. Extension cords should be covered with Type SJT insulation, and have molded-on weatherproof plugs and sockets. Underground wiring should be done with Type USE or UF cables. These can be laid directly in the ground; but should be run through conduits under paved areas so they can be replaced, or so you can add cables without digging up the paving. All outlets, switches, and lampholders must also be weatherproof.

The lights most commonly used outdoors are PAR incandescent bulbs. Designed either for floodlighting or spotlighting, these are made with heavy, heat-resistant glass which can be exposed directly to the weather. For most purposes, 75-watt bulbs are best, although the 150-watt size is used quite often.

When less wattage is needed, use ordinary household bulbs. Sizes up to 25 watts can be exposed to the weather since they do not generate enough heat to break when splattered with rain or snow. Above 25 watts, however, the bulbs must be completely protected from the weather.

Fixtures of many designs are available. Some are decorative; some, strictly utilitarian. I prefer the utilitarian because they are low in cost, and easy to install and conceal. The simplest fixture is nothing more than an adjustable, weatherproof lampholder, or socket. This serves most purposes when the lights can be hidden in shrubbery, behind a tree trunk or in a similar location. But when concealment is difficult, or when it is necessary to concentrate the beam of light, I use weatherproof, adjustable, bullet-type fixtures.

Basic rules for lighting the winter garden

1. Do not use too much light. In the first place, you don't need very many watts of light to make a dent in the darkness. In the second place, there is something magic and mysterious about the darkness of a garden at night which is easily destroyed if you use too much light.

The aim in using light in a garden is not to turn night into day, but to enhance the beauty of the night.

2. Be restrained in the picture you paint. Don't be tricky. Consider the shape, texture, outline, and size of whatever you are lighting, and light it in the simplest way you can.

3. Don't aim any light so it shines into the windows of neighboring houses.

4. Use white light only. It produces the most nearly natural effect, brings out the colors of the garden best. Colored light is very occasionally effective in the summer garden; and part of the reason for this is that we expect color in summer. But in the very subdued, neutral setting of the winter garden, colored light is too unreal.

5. Place each light so that the bulb is concealed from direct view. There are many ways to do this: Hide the light in evergreen foliage or in the branches of a tree; or mount it on the roof so you can see it only if you are walking in the garden (which you don't often do on winter nights). Use it in a bullet reflector. Recess it in a large tin can, flower pot or drainage tile sunk in the ground.

How to light trees

Deciduous trees lend themselves better to lighting than any other garden element. This is true in both summer and winter. You may not light them in the same way in the two seasons, however; that depends on the structure of the tree, the density of the foliage, and the end you wish to achieve.

Probably the most dramatic way to light a tree in winter is from the ground up. This is certainly the best way if the tree has an unusually handsome crown or interesting branch structure. It is also the best way if a tree is growing at a distance from the house. For a natural effect, however, trees should be lighted from the top down so that they appear to be under a full moon. This is a particularly good lighting method if a tree is close to the house, and if the ground underneath is smooth enough for the shadows cast by the limbs to show up clearly.

Whether lighting a tree from below or above, avoid lighting it head-on, because the effect is flat and the texture of the trunk is likely to be washed out. You get better modeling by lighting from two angles; and for the best effect, one light should be stronger than the other.

Another effective way to bring out the structure of a tree, is to place the lights behind it and let the beams just graze off the branches. If a tree with a good trunk or branch structure is planted in front of a wall, play the lights on the wall so the tree stands out in silhouette. In both cases, you should also direct a little light on the front of the tree.

Very open conifers, such as a Tanyosho Pine, are lighted like deciduous species. Most conifers and broadleaf evergreens, however, have such dense foliage that light directed into them is lost. The best way to light them is to place lights on the ground around them and graze the light off the tips of the branches. Small, shapely plants can be silhouetted against a wall.

How to light shrubs

Like trees, deciduous shrubs usually look better lighted than everygreens. In all cases, however, shrubs are most effective when you silhouette them against a lighted background and direct a small amount of light at them from the front or side. Bamboo, Heavenly Bamboo, Enkianthus and *Euonymus alatus* are particularly appealing when lighted this way.

Shrubs, trees and vines which are espaliered on a wall are also beautiful under light; but the lighting is difficult to arrange. If using PAR or household bulbs, place two lights of equal but low intensity in front of, and to the sides of, the plant so that the shadows cast by the branches against the wall are washed out, and so that the wall itself does not appear glary. The alternative—more expensive but better—is to install a fluorescent outdoor fixture on the ground right in front of the plant and aim it upward.

How to light garden sculpture

Because most sculpture is light-colored, use relatively low-wattage bulbs. For instance, you can spotlight or floodlight a piece from some distance with two 75-watt PAR bulbs; or you can light it closer up with 25- or 40-watt household bulbs in reflectors. The real key to successful lighting of sculpture, however, is the placement of the bulbs. Try to bring out the form and texture of the piece; don't just illuminate it.

This means that you should rarely direct just one light on a piece of sculpture: That makes it look one-sided. You need two or three lights aimed from different angles. One, perhaps, is a spotlight to accent certain features; the others are floodlights that provide general illumination without destroying the shadow pattern.

How to create an overall effect

Obviously, when you are lighting a garden, you should not just light a tree here, a shrub there, a statue somewhere else. Your aim must be to create a picture with unity, balance, depth, and a focal point. This doesn't mean you must install a great many lights; on the contrary, the lighting of a single tree with just a couple of lights may be all the picture you need. But the only way you can determine what should be done is to experiment for several nights.

The focal point of the scene should be the most brightly lighted element in the garden. Ideally, it should be lighted so that it pulls the eye upward to the black sky. But it should not appear to be isolated from other lighted elements. In other words, it should not be surrounded by complete darkness.

This is also true of other lighted elements. You should strive for an interplay, or mixture, of light and shadow throughout the lighted part of the garden, but jet black spots between elements must be avoided since they tend to fragment the overall picture.

Straight rows of lights, and very large expanses of light of the same intensity (as on a long wall, for instance), should also be avoided. The well-lighted garden is informal, although all lighted areas should be in balance.

How to enjoy the lighted garden from inside the house

Obviously, there is no sense in lighting the winter garden if you cannot enjoy it from indoors. But here we run up against a problem: Seated in a lighted room, it is impossible to see outside because the windows are black, impenetrable mirrors. This is true of all windows, but especially so of picture windows because the glass expanse is large and unbroken.

Lighting a garden outside a window helps to relieve the situation because the lights make the glass transparent. But the picture of the garden which you see is confused by the reflections in the window of the interior furnishings. Luckily, there are several things you can do to correct matters:

Raise the light level in the garden by illuminating the entire area seen from indoors with several 150-watt PAR floodlights. These should be installed on the house 2 ft. or more above the corners of the windows through which you view the garden. Aim them across the window at 45 degree angles. Since this tends to flatten the light on the garden, you should then increase the intensity of the lights directed at trees, shrubs and sculpture.

Equip lamps in the room or rooms overlooking the garden with opaque lampshades, and position the lamps so that their reflections are not visible in the windows.

Lower the light level in the room.

John Watson of Dallas, the country's outstanding outdoor lighting expert, created this pleasant scene with a few flood-lights aimed up into the trees and down from the high limbs. The little statue is lighted from two sides to bring out its lines.

These trees are lighted by floods directed up from the ground.

PHOTO BY GENERAL ELECTRIC

Overall lighting of this winter scene comes from a 100-watt PAR floodlight in a bullet fixture mounted in a tree out of view to the left. Highlights on the small tree in the background are created by a floodlight recessed in the ground at the base of the trunk.

Flowing water brings interest to the garden at all hours of the day and is especially exciting when lighted at night.

The full value of outdoor lighting is realized only if you can enjoy the scene you create from a comfortable chair indoors. This calls for careful placement of lights both outside and inside to make windows transparent. For instructions on doing this, see the text. PHOTO BY GENERAL ELECTRIC

Index

Note: Numbers in italics indicate illustrations.

Abies concolor, 29, *53*; A. *homolepis*, 29, *54*
Acer circinatum, 124; A. *griseum*, 29, *55*; A. *japonicum*, 31; A. *palmatum*, 31, *220*; A. *platanoides*, 31, *56*; A. *saccharum*, 32, *57*; A. *sieboldianum*, 32, *58*
Aconite, Winter, 179
Adonis amurensis, 176
Albizia julibrissin, 32
Andromeda, Japanese, 85, 135, *163*, *164*; Mountain, 125, *162*
Anemone blanda, 177
Apple, 42, 85
Arborvitae, American, 5, 12, 51, *157*; Giant, 51
Arbutus menziesii, 33; A. *unedo*, 124
Arctostaphylos uva-ursi, 124, *140*
Aucuba japonica variegata, 125, *141*
Azalea, 137

Bamboo, 12; Chinese Goddess, 125; Palmate, 137, *165*; Yellow-groove, 136, *166*

Bambusa multiplex riviercorum, 125
Barberry, Chenault, 125, *140*; Warty, 125; Wintergreen, 125, *142*
Bark, tree, 26
Basswood, 52
Bearberry, 124, *140*
Beech, 26; American, 38, *69*; European, 38, *70*, *71*
Bent Grass, 190
Berberis chenaultii, 125, *140*; B. *julianae*, 125, *142*; B. *verruculosa*, 125
Bergenia ligulata, 176
Bermuda Grass, 188
Betula papyrifera, 33, *59*; B. *pendula*, 26, 34, *60*
Birdhouses, 194
Birch, canoe, 33, *59*; European, 26, 34, *60*; Gray, 33; Paper, 33, *59*; White, 33, *59*
Birds, 193; feeding of, 198; houses for, 194; plants giving shelter to, 195; roosting boxes, 198; trees and shrubs as food for, 200; water for, 194

239

Black Alder, 132, *154*
Blue Beech, 34, *61*
Blueberry, Highbush, 138, *171*
Bluegrass, 190
Boxwood, 12; Common, *15*, *16*, 126, *142*
Brick walls, 211
Broom, Warminster, 128, *145*
Buckthorn, Sea, 131
Bulbocodium vernum, 177
Bulbs, 177
Bull Bay, 41, *82*
Burningbush, 129, *147*
Buxus sempervirens, 12, *15*, *16*, 126, *142*

Camellia, Common, 126, 174, *182*; Sasanqua, 126, 174
Camellia japonica, 126, 174, *182*; *C. sasanqua*, 126, 174
Carpinus betulus columnaris, 34, *63*; *C. caroliniana*, 34, *61*
Carya illinoensis, 34; *C. ovata*, 35, *62*
Cedar, Atlas, 35; Deodar, 35, *62*; of Lebanon, 35, *63*
Cedrus atlantica, 35; *C. deodara*, 35, *62*; *C. libani*, 35, *63*
Chamaecyparis lawsoniana ellwoodii, 35; *C. obtusa*, 36; *C. pisifera*, 6, 36, *76*; *C. pisifera squarrosa*, 36, *64*, *76*
Cherry, Oriental, 47, *103*
Chimonanthus praecox, 126, *183*
Chionodoxa luciliae, 178
Christmas Rose, 176, *186*
Cladrastis lutea, 36, *65*
Cloth of Gold, 178
Concrete block walls, 210
Concrete walls, 210
Cork Tree, Amur, 12, 43, *88*
Cornus alba sibirica, 127, *143*; *C. florida*, *15*, 36, *66*; *C. kousa*, 37, *67*

Corylus avellana contorta, 127, *144*
Cotoneaster, Bearberry, 128, *145*; Necklace, 127; Pyrenees, 127; Redbox, 128; Rockspray, 128
Cotoneaster congesta, 127; *C. conspicua decora*, 127; *C. dammeri*, 128, *145*; *C. lactea*, 128; *C. microphylla*, 128; *C. rotundifolia*, 128
Crabapple, Tea, 42, *84*
Crape Myrtle, 40, *79*
Crataegus phaenopyrum, 37, *68*
Crocus aureus, 178; *C. biflorus*, 178; *C. chrysanthus*, 178; *C. imperati*, 178; *C. longiflorus*, 178; *C. sieberi atticus*, 178; *C. susianus*, 178; *C. tomasinianus*, 178
Cyclamen atkinsii, 179
Cytisus praecox, 128, *145*

Daphne cneorum, 128
Daphne, Rose, 128
Dawn Redwood, 42, *86*
Diospyros kaki, 37, *68*
Dogwood, Evergreen, *141*; Flowering, *15*, 36, *66*; Japanese, 37, *67*; Korean, 37, *67*, Siberian, 127, *143*
Driftwood, 216

Elaeagnus angustifolia, 37, *71*
Elm, American, 52, *121*
Enkianthus campanulatus, 129
Enkianthus, Redvein, 129
Eranthis hyemalis, 179
Erica carnea, 129, *146*
Euonymus alatus, 129, *147*; *E. fortunei*, 130, *148*; *E. japonicus*, *16*, 130
Euonymus, Japanese, *16*, 130; Winged, 129, *147*

Fagus grandifolia, 38, 69; *F. sylvatica*, 38, 70, 71
False Cypress, Ellwood, 35; Hinoki, 36; Moss, 36, *64, 76*; Sawara, *6*, 36, *76*
Fatshedera, 130, *149*
Fatshedera lizei, 130, *149*
Fatsia, Japanese, 130, *148*
Fatsia japonica, 130, *148*
Fences, 212–13
Fescue, 189, 190
Fir, Nikko, 29, *54;* White, 29, *53*
Firethorn, 136, *168*
Flowers, 173; establishing conditions for, 174

Galanthus elwesii, 179, *185*
Gazebos, 214
Ginkgo, 38, 72
Ginkgo biloba, 38, 72
Gleditsia triacanthos inermis, 11, 38, 73
Glory of the Snow, 178
Gold-Dust plant, 125, *141*
Grass, 187; Bent, 190; Bermuda, 188; Blue, 190; Fescue, 189, 190; Rye, 188, 190; Zoysia, 188
Ground Pine, 134, *159*
Gum, Black, 42, 87; Sour, 42, 87

Hamamelis mollis, 131, *183; H. vernalis*, 131, *184*
Harry Lauder's Walking Stick, 127, *144*
Heath, Spring, 129, *146*
Heather, *146*
Heavenly Bamboo, 135, *160*
Hedera helix, 21, 131, *150*
Hedges, 13, 174
Heliotrope, Winter, 177
Hellebores, 174, 175
Helleborus foetidus, 176; *H. niger*, 176, *186; H. orientalis*, 176
Hemlock, 11; Canada, 21, 22, 52,

148; Carolina, 52, *120;* Sargent's Weeping, 22, 52, 90
Hickory, Shagbark, 35, *62*, 203
Hippophae rhamnoides, 131
Holly, American, *16*, 39, *76, 152–153;* Chinese, *16*, 132, *151;* Convex Japanese, 11, *66, 74*, 132, *158;* English, 39, *74;* Heller's, 132, *152–153;* Longstalk, 39, *77;* Lusterleaf, 39, *75*
Honeylocust, Thornless, 11, 38, *73*
Hornbeam, American, 34, *61;* Columnar European, 34, *63*
Hyacinthus azureus, 179

Ilex aquifolium, 39, *74; I. cornuta*, *16*, 132, *151; I. crenata convexa*, 11, *66, 74*, 132; *I. crenata helleri*, 132, *152–153; I. latifolia*, 39, *75; I. opaca*, *16*, 39, *76*, *152–153; I. peduncusola*, 39, *77; I. verticillata*, 132, *154; I. vomitoria*, 40, *75*
Iris bakeriana, 179; *I. danfordiae*, 179; *I. histrioides major*, 180; *I. reticulata*, 180
Ironwood, 34, *61*
Ivy, English, *21*, 131, *150*

Juniper, Creeping, 133, *156;* Meyer, 133, *157;* Pfitzer, 132, *155;* Rocky Mountain, 40; Sargent, 132, *155;* Shore, 132; Tamarix, 133; Waukegan, *156*
Juniperus chinensis pfitzeriana, 132, *155; J. chinensis sargentii*, 132, *155; J. communis compressa*, 132; *J. conferta*, 132; *J. horizontalis*, 132, *156; J. procumbens nana*, 133; *J. sabina tamariscifolia*, 133; *J. scopulorum*, 40; *J. squamata meyeri*, 133, *157; J. virginiana*, 40, *78*, *85*

Kalmia latifolia, 133, *157*, *158*
Kinnikinnick (Bearberry), 124,
    140

Lagerstroemia indica, 40, 79
Larch, Weeping European, 40, *80*
Larix decidua pendula, 40, *80*
Lawns, 14, 187; dying, 188; heat-
    ing, 189; in Zone 8, 188; syn-
    thetic turf, 190
Leaves, 10, 13
Lenten Rose, 176
Leucojum vernum, 180
Leucothoe, Drooping, 66, 133
Leucothoe fontanesiana, 66, 133
Lighting, 228; basic rules, 230;
    equipment, 229; garden sculp-
    ture, 233; shrubs and, 232;
    trees and, 231; picture-window
    problems and, 234
Ligustrum japonicum, 134, *158*
Lily-of-the-valley shrub, 85, 135,
    163, *164*
Linden, American, 52, *118–119*
Liriodendron tulipifera, 41, *81*
Locust, Black, 26, 28
Lungwort, Cowslip, 177
Lycopodium obscurum, 134, *159*

Madrone, Pacific, 33
Magnolia, grandiflora, 41, *82*; *M.
    soulangeana*, 41, *83*
Magnolia, Saucer, 41, *83*; South-
    ern, 41, *82*
Mahonia aquifolium, 134, *159*; *M.
    bealei*, 134, *160*
Mahonia, Leatherleaf, 134, *160*
Malus hupehensis, 42, *84*; *M. pu-
    mila*, 42, *85*
Maple, Fullmoon, 31; Japanese,
    31, *220*; Norway, 31, *56*, 203;
    Paperbark, 29, *55*; Siebold, 32,
    58; Sugar, 32, *57*; Vine, 124
Metasequoia glyptostroboides, 42,
    86

Mimosa, 32
Mountain Ash, Korean, 50, *115*
Mountain Laurel, 133, *157*; Com-
    pact, *158*
Myrtle, 139

Nandina domestica, 135, *160*
Narcissus asturiensis, 180; *N. cy-
    clamineus*, 180
Nylon synthetic turf, 191
Nyssa sylvatica, 42, *87*

Oak, Black, 26, 49, *110*; California
    White, 48; Canyon Live, 48;
    Cork, 49, *109*; Laurel, 48, *106*;
    Live, 49, *111*; Pin, 5, 48; red,
    48, *108*, 203; Shingle, 48, *106*;
    Swamp White, 47, *105*; Valley,
    48; White, 11, 12, 47, *104*, 203;
    Willow, 48, *107*
Oregon Grape, 134, *159*
Osmanthus heterophyllus, 135, *161*
Osmanthus, Holly, 135, *161*

Pachysandra, *142*
Pacific Madrone, 33
Paxistima canbyi, 135, *162*
Pecan, 34, 203
Pepperidge, 42, *87*
Perennials, 176
Periwinkle, 139
Persimmon, Japanese, 37, *68*; Ori-
    ental, 37, *68*
Petasites fragrans, 177
Phellodendron amurense, 12, 43,
    88
Photinia, Fraser, 136, *167*
Photinia fraseri, 136, *167*
Phyllostachys aureosulcata, 136,
    166
Picea abies, 43, *89*; *P. engelman-
    nii*, 43; *P. glauca conica*, 43, *90*;
    P. omorika, 44, *91*
Pierced walls, 211

Pieris floribunda, 135, *162*; *P. japonica*, 85, 135, *163*, *164*
Pine, Austrian, 45, 97; Bristlecone, 44, *92*; Coulter, 44; Eastern White, 22, 46, 87, *101*, *156*; Himalayan, 45, *92*; Japanese Black, 47, *102*; Japanese Red, 44, 95; Korean, 45, *96*; Lacebark, 44, *93*; Loblolly, *167*; Longleaf, 45, *98*; Mugo, 136, *165*; Norway, 46, *83*; Ponderosa, 46, *99*; Red, 46, *83*; Scotch, 46, 60, *102*; Swiss Stone, 44, *94*; Table Mountain, 46, *100*; Western White, 45
Pinus aristata, 44, *92*; *P. bungeana*, 44, *93*; *P. cembra*, 44, *94*; *P. coulter*, 44; *P. densiflora*, 44, 95; *P. griffiithii*, 45, *92*; *P. koraiensis*, 45, *96*; *P. monticola*, 45; *P. mugo mughus*, 136, *165*; *P. nigra*, 45, *97*; *P. palustris*, 45, *98*; *P. ponderosa*, 46, *99*; *P. pungens*, 46, *100*; *P. resinosa*, 46; *P. strobus*, 22, 46, 87, *101*, *156*; *P. sylvestris*, 46, 60, *102*; *P. thunbergii*, 47, *102*
Podocarpus macrophylla maki, 136
Podocarpus, Yew, 136
Polyethylene synthetic turf, 191
Pools, 10
Poplar, Tulip, 41, *81*; Yellow, 41, *81*
Primula denticulata, 177
Privet, Japanese, 134, *158*
Prunus serrulata washino-o, 47, *103*
Pulmonaria angustifolia, 177
Pyracantha coccinea lalandii, 136, *168*

Quercus alba, 11, 12, 47, *104*; *Q. bicolor*, 47, *105*; *Q. chrysolepis*, 48; *Q. imbricaria*, 48, *106*; *Q. lobata*, 48; *Q. palustris*, 5, 48;

Q. phellos, 48, *107*; *Q. rubra*, 48, *108*; *Q. suber*, 49, *109*; *Q. velutina*, 26, 49, *110*; *Q. virginiana*, 49, *111*

Red Cedar, Eastern, 40, 78, 85; Western, 40
Rhododendron, 66, 112, 137
Rose gardens, 10
Russian Olive, 37, *71*
Rye Grass, 188, 190

Saffron, Spring Meadow, 177
Salix alba tristis, 49; *S. babylonica*, 50, *112*; *S. elegantissima*, 50; *S. matsudana tortuosa*, 50, *113*
Sasa palmata, 137, *165*
Sassafras, 28
Sciadopitys verticillata, 50, *114*
Scilla bifolia, 180; *S. sibirica*, 180; *S. tubergeniana*, 180
Sculpture, garden, 214–16
Shrubs, 22, 200
Silk Tree, 32
Skimmia, Reeves, 138
Skimmia reevesiana, 138
Sloping land, 9
Snowdrop, 179, *185*
Snowflake, 180
Snow, effect of, 4, 5; soot on snow, 14
Sorbus alnifolia, 50, *115*
Spruce, Engelmann, 43; Dwarf White, 43, 90; Norway, 43, 89; 44, 91
Squirrels, 202
Stewartia, Japanese, 51; Korean, 51, *116*
Stewartia koreana, 51, *116*; *S. pseudocamellia*, 50
Stones for ornament, 217
Stone walls, 211
Stranvaesia davidiana, 138, *169*
Strawberry Tree, 124

Sycamore, 6, 28, *164*
Synthetic turf, 190–92

Taxus baccata stricta, 11, 12, 51, *117*; *T. cuspidata*, 15, 138; *T. media hatfieldii*, 51; *T. media hicksii*, 51, *117*
Ternstroemia gymnanthera, 138, *170*
Thorn, Washington, 37, *68*
Thuja occidentalis, 5, 12, 51, *157*; *T. plicata*, 51
Tilia americana, 52, *118–19*
Trafficways, 14
Trees, 11, 26, 200
Tsuga canadensis, 11, 21, 22, 52, 90, *148*; *T. canadensis pendula*, 22, 52, 90; *T. caroliniana*, 52, *120*
Tulipa kaufmanniana, 180; *T. pulchella violacea*, 181
Tulip Tree, 41, *81*
Tulip, Water Lily, 180
Tupelo, 42, 87

Ulmus americana, 52, *121*
Umbrella Pine, 50, *114*

Vaccinium corymbosum, 138, *171*
Viburnum, Leatherleaf, 139, *172*
Viburnum rhytidophyllum, 139, *172*

Vinca minor, 139
Vines, 122

Walls, 5, 14, 174, 208, 209–12
Willow, Babylon Weeping, 50, *112*; Corkscrew, 50, *113*; Golden Weeping, 49; Thurlow Weeping, 50
Wind, 13, 174
Windflower, Sapphire, 177
Winter garden, the focal points in, 13; form in, importance of, 10–12; landscaping of, 7–25; lawns and (*see* Lawns); lighting and (*see* Lighting); location of, 8–9; obstacles in, 9–10; sculpture for, 214–16; swimming pools and, 10; viewing, 8, 9, 12–14; walls and, 209–12
Winterberry, 132, *154*
Wintercreeper, 130, *148*
Wintersweet, 126, *183*
Witchhazel, Chinese, 131, *183*; Vernal, 131, *184*

Yaupon, 40, 75
Yellow-wood, 36, *65*
Yew, Hatfield, 51; Hicks, 51, *117*; Irish, 11, 12, 51, *117*; Japanese, 15, 138
Yew Pine, Shrubby, 136

Zoysia, 188